A Straightforward Guide to

CRIMINAL LAW

First Edition

Philip G. Cowburn

LL.B. (Hons), LL.M., Barrister, F.Inst.Pa., FHEA, MCMI, MInstLM, CMBE.

With a Guest Chapter by Carley Lightfoot, LL.B. (Hons), LL.M.

Editor: Roger Sproston
Author Support: Jennifer Warrington

Straightforward Publishing
www.straightforwardbooks.co.uk

Copyright First Edition © Philip G. Cowburn 2023

Philip G. Cowburn has asserted the moral right to be identified as the author of this work.

All rights reserved. No part of this publication may be reproduced in a retrieval system or transmitted by any means, electronic or mechanical, photocopying or otherwise, without the prior permission of the copyright holders.

ISBN 978-1-80236-187-2

Printed by 4edge www.4edge.co.uk
Text layout by Frabjous Books

Whilst every effort has been made to ensure that the information contained within this book is correct at the time of going to press, the author and publisher can take no responsibility for any errors or omissions contained within.

Contains public sector information licensed under the Open Government Licence v3.0.

For Mum & Dad
Philip Gordon Cowburn

Chapter Eleven for N'kose
Carley Lightfoot

CONTENTS

Preface		vii
Table of Cases		ix
Table of Statues		xiv
Chapter 1	How the Criminal Justice System Works	1
Chapter 2	Defining Crime	11
Chapter 3	Fatal Offences Against the Person	27
Chapter 4	Non-Fatal Offences Against the Person	45
Chapter 5	Sexual Offences	55
Chapter 6	Theft, Fraud, and Related Offences	69
Chapter 7	Damage to Property	91
Chapter 8	Drug Offences	97
Chapter 9	Offences against Public Order	105
Chapter 10	Driving and Road Traffic Offences	115
Chapter 11	Offences involving Animals	123
Chapter 12	Offences involving Technology	141
Chapter 13	General Defences	147
Further Reading & Online Resources		155
Index		157

PREFACE

A Straightforward Guide to Criminal Law aims to introduce the reader, be they student or not, to the fundamentals of Criminal Law.

It is intended that this straightforward guide should make concepts that are ordinarily reserved for those studying Criminal Law in formal settings, accessible to a wider audience. It considers key case law and relevant statutes – it does not, and could not, provide the full picture; I therefore encourage readers to use this text as an introductory springboard – to further reading or study. I include some texts that I personally recommend to students at the end of this text.

I take this opportunity to thank my friend Carley Lightfoot for her contribution, which takes the form of Chapter Eleven in this text. Animal Crime is a growing area of criminal law, and, with further advances in the socio-legal study of animal sentience, it is likely that Carley's wider work will make a real impact on the laws of the future.

I also wish to extend my thanks to Roger, my publisher and editor, and to Jen for her assistance with the technical administration required of a legal text of this nature, their advice and support has been fundamental to the completion of this text. Also, my family, friends and professional colleagues for all you do.

All efforts have been made to ensure the accuracy of the material contained within this text. This book is not, and should not be treated as, legal advice. Criminal law is a complicated subject matter; any persons facing a criminal charge, or the prospect of such a charge, should seek advice from a qualified, and insured, legal professional specialising in Criminal Defence.

I have made every effort to ensure the accuracy of this text, any mistakes are my own and feedback is always welcome. Further resources may be posted to my website (https://www.cowburn.pro/sgcl).

This book was finalised on 3rd April 2023 and is, as far as possible, intended to reflect the law, as at that date.

Philip Gordon Cowburn
3 April 2023

TABLE OF CASES

A-G's Ref (No.1 of 1983) [1985] QB 182 75
Airedale NHS Trust v Bland [1983] AC 789 29
Bandeira and Brannigan v RSPCA (2000) CO 2066/99 127
Barnet LBC v Eastern Electricity Board [1973] 1 WLR 430 93
Boldizsar v Knight [1980] Crim LR 653 89
Brown v Fisk & Ors [2021] EWHC 2769 (QB) 119
Burrell v Hammer [1967] Crim LR 169 151
Collins v Wilcock [1984] 3 All ER 374 48
Donaghy and Marshall [1981] Crim LR 644 78
DPP v Barreto [2019] EWHC 2044 (Admin) 118–121
DPP v Brooks [1974] AC 862 99
DPP v Catcher (1992) The Times, 29 December 1992 109
DPP v Distill [2017] EWHC 2244 (Admin) 112
DPP v Parker [1989] RTR 413 121
DPP v Percy [2001] All ER (D) 387 (Dec) 114
DPP v Smith [1961] AC 290 50
DPP v Smith [2017] EWHC 3193 (Admin) 113
Ford v Wiley [1889] 23 QBD 203 129
Hammond v DPP [2004] EWHC 69 (Admin) 114
Hardman v Chief Constable of Avon and Somerset Constabulary
   [1986] Crim LR 330 93
Haystead v Chief Constable of Derbyshire [2000] 3 All ER 890 46
Hutchinson v DPP (2000) Independent, 20 November 2000 93
I v DPP [2001] UKHL 10 108
Ireland v Burstow [1998] AC 147 46
Ivey v Genting Casinos (UK) Ltd t/a Crockfords [2018] AC 391 72
JCC (a minor) v Eisenhower [1984] QB 331 51
Leeson v DPP [2010] EWHC 994 (Admin) 109
Lloyd v DPP [1992] 1 All ER 982 93
Logdon v DPP [1976] Crim LR 121 46
Low v Blease [1975] Crim LR 513 74
Moriarty v Brooks (1834) 6 C&P 684 51
Morphitis v Salmon [1990] Crim LR 48 93

Mundi v Warwickshire Police [2001] EWHC Admin 448 121
Norwood v DPP [2003] EWHC 1564 (Admin) 114
P v DPP [2013] 1 WLR 2337 77
Pwr v DPP [2022] 1 WLR 789 25
R (DPP) v Humphrey [2005] EWHC 822 (Admin) 111
R (Nicklinson) v Ministry of Justice [2012] EWHC 2381 (Admin) .. 29
R (Nicklinson) v Ministry of Justice [2013] EWCA Civ 961 29
R (Nicklinson) v Ministry of Justice [2015] AC 657 29
R (on the application of Gray and another) v Aylesbury Crown
  Court [2013] EWHC 500 (Admin) 130
R (on the application of Ricketts) v Basildon Magistrates' Court
  [2010] EWHC 2358 (Admin) 74
R (RSPCA) v C [2006] EWHC 1069 (Admin) 139
R v Adebelajo [2014] EWCA Crim 2779 30
R v Adomako [1995] 1 AC 171 40
R v Aitken [1992] 1 WLR 1066 152
R v Allen [1985] AC 1029 87
R v Ambrose (1973) 57 Cr App R 538 111
R v Aziz [1993] Crim LR 708 86
R v Barton and Booth [2020] EWCA Crim 575 72
R v Bateman (1925) 19 Cr App R 8 40
R v Bignell [1998] 1 Cr App R 1 144
R v Billinghurst [1978] Crim LR 553 152
R v Birmingham [2002] EWCA Crim 2608 51
R v Blackburn [1968] 2 Q.B. 118 2
R v Blaue (Kenneth Joseph) [1975] 3 All ER 446 20
R v Bogacki [1973] QB 832 88
R v Bollom [204] 2 Cr App R 50 50
R v Bounekhla [2006] EWCA Crim 1217 66
R v Bow Street Magistrates' Court and Allison (AP) Ex Parte
  Government of the United States of America (Allison) [2002]
  2 AC 216 144
R v Braham [2013] EWCA Crim 3 62
R v Broughton [2021] 1 Cr App R 3 40
R v Brown (Vincent) [1985] Crim LR 212 79
R v Brown [1993] 2 All ER 75 153
R v Byrne [1960] 2 QB 396 36

TABLE OF CASES

R v C [2012] EWCA Crim 2034 58
R v Caldwell [1982] AC 341 24
R v Carey [2006] EWCA Crim 17 39
R v Church [1966] 1 QB 59 39
R v Clinton [2013] QB 1 33
R v Clouden [1987] Crim LR 56 77
R v Collins [1973] QB 100 79
R v Constanza [1997] 2 Cr App R 492 47
R v Cooksley [2003] EWCA Crim 996 118
R v Cunningham [1957] 2 QB 396 23
R v Davison [1992] Crim LR 31 106
R v Dawson (1976) 64 Cr App R 170 77
R v Dhaliwal [2006] EWCA Crim 1139 50
R v Diggin (1980) 72 Cr App R 204 89
R v Dixon [1993] Crim LR 579 108
R v DM [2023] EWCA Crim 150 128
R v Dowds [2012] 1 Cr App R 34 36
R v F [2002] EWCA Crim 2936 57
R v Francis [2007] 1 WLR 1021 112
R v G [2004] 1 AC 1034 24
R v Gibbins and Proctor (1918) 12 Cr App R 134 17
R v Gilbert [2012] EWCA Crim 2392 131
R v Golds [2017] 1 Cr App R 18 37
R v Gomez [1993] AC 442 43
R v Gurpinar [2015] 1 Cr App R 31 32
R v H [2005] 1 WLR 2005 64
R v Hood [2004] 1 Cr App R (S) 73 17
R v Hughes [2013] UKSC 56 19
R v Inglis [210] EWCA Crim 2637 29
R v Instan [1893] 1 QB 450 15
R v Ireland & Burstow [1998] AC 147 147
R v Ireland [1998] AC 147 52
R v Isted [1998] 162 J.P. 513 128
R v Jeshani [2005] EWCA Crim 146 118
R v Jewell (Darren) [2014] EWCA Crim 414 33
R v Jones (John) [1976] 3 All ER 54 81
R v Kato [1998] 4 All ER 417 119

R v Kelly [1999] QB 621 74
R v Lamb [1967] 2 QB 981 39
R v Lambert [2002] AC 545 99
R v Lindo [2016] EWCA Crim 1940 36
R v Loukes [1996] 1 Cr App R 444 116
R v M'Loughlin (1838) 8 C&P 635 51
R v Maginnis [1987] AC 303 102
R v Marsh [2002] EWCA Crim 137 118
R v Martin (Dwain) & Anor [2015] 1 WLR 588 102
R v McDavitt [1981] Crim LR 843 87
R v McInnes [1971] 3 All ER 295 151
R v Miller [1954] 2 QB 282 49
R v Miller [1983] 2 AC 161 14-18
R v Misra [2005] 1 Cr App R 21 41
R v Mitchell [1983] QB 741 19
R v Mitchell [2008] EWCA Crim 850 76
R v Nica [2021] EWCA Crim 1790 38
R v Nicholls (1874) 13 Cox CC 75 15
R v Nixon [2020] EWCA Crim 336 33
R v Olugboja [1982] QB 320 62
R v Pagett (Keith David) (1983) 76 Cr. App. R. 279 21-28
R v Pearce (1973)Crim LR 321 89
R v Pittwood (1902) 19 TLR 37 16
R v Poulton (1832) 5 C&P 329 30
R v Prior [2004] EWCA Crim 1147 103
R v Renouf [1986] 2 All ER 449 148
R v Richardson [1998] 2 Cr App R 200 152
R v Roberts (1972) 56 CR. App. R. 95 21
R v Robinson [1977] Crim LR 173 77
R v Smith (Christopher Floyd) [1997] 1 Cr App R 14 107
R v Smith (Michael Andrew) [2011] EWCA Crim 66 74
R v Smith (Thomas Joseph) [1959] 2 QB 35 20
R v Smith [1979] Crim LR 251 67
R v Steer [1988] AC 111 111
R v Stokes [1983] RTR 59 89
R v Strong [1995] Crim LR 428 118
R v Symonds [1998] Crim LR 280 148

TABLE OF CASES

R v Tabassum [2000] 2 Cr App R 328 152
R v Thakar [2010] EWCA Crim 2136 95
R v Thind [1999] Crim LR 842 107
R v Thomas (1985) 81 Cr App R 331 48
R v Walkington [1979] 2 All ER 716 80
R v Waltham (1849) 3 Cox CC 442 41
R v White [1910] 2 KB 124 19
R v Whitley (1991) 93 Cr App R 25 94
R v Wilcocks [2017] 1 Cr App R 23 35
R v Williams (Gladstone) [1987] 3 All ER 411 48
R v Wilson [1996] Crim LR 573 152
R v Woolin [1999] AC 82 31
R v Wright [2011] Cr App R 15 104
R(R) v DPP [2006] EWHC 1375 (Admin) 110
Re A (Children) (Conjoined twins: surgical separation) [2001]
    4 All ER 961 30
Riley v Crown Prosecution Service [2016] EWHC 2531 (Admin) .. 131
RSPCA v McCormick [2016] EWHC 928 (Admin) 137
Smith v Chief Constable of Woking Police Station (1983) 76 Cr
    App R 234 47
Southern Water Authority v Pegrum [1989] Crim LR 442 22
Stevens v Gourley (1859) CBNS 99 80
Tracey v DPP [1971] AC 537 84
Waller v CPS [2018] EWHC 3303 (Admin) 121
Wright v Reading Crown Court [2017] EWHC 2643 (Admin) 137

TABLE OF STATUTES

Animal Welfare Act 2006

S1	125
S1(1)	125
S1(2)	125
S2	125
S2(a)	125
S2(b)	125
S2(c)	125
S3	126
S3(1)	126
S3(2)	126
S3(3)	126
S3(4)	126
S4	126
S4(1)	127, 128
S4(1)(a)	127
S4(1)(b)	127
S4(1)(c)	127
S4(1)(d)	127
S4(2)	130
S4(2)(a)	130
S4(2)(b)	131
S4(2)(c)	131
S4(2)(d)	131
S4(3)	129
S4(3)(a)	129
S4(3)(b)	129
S4(3)(c)	129
S4(3)(d)	129
S4(3)(e)	129
S5	131
S5(2)	132
S5(3)	131
S6	221
S6(1)	221
S6(2)	132
S7	132
S7(1)	132, 133
S7(1)(a)	133
S7(1)(b)	133
S7(2)	132, 133
S7(2)(a)	133
S7(2)(b)	133
S7(2)(c)	133
S8	134
S8(1)	135
S8(1)(a)	135
S8(1)(b)	135
S8(1)(c)	135
S8(1)(d)	135
S8(1)(e)	135
S8(1)(f)	135
S8(1)(g)	135
S8(1)(h)	135
S8(1)(i)	135
S8(2)	135, 136
S8(3)	135, 136
S8(3)(a)	135, 136
S8(3)(b)	135, 136
S8(3)(c)	135, 136
S8(3)(d)	137
S8(5)	136
S8(7)	134
S62	127
S62(1)	137

TABLE OF STATUTES

Animal Welfare Act 2009..... 137
S4 117
S4(1) 117
S9 .... 137, 138
S9(1) 138
S9(2) 138
S9(2)(a) 139
S9(2)(b) 139
S9(2)(c) 139
S9(2)(d) 139
S9(2)(e) 138
S9(3) 138
S9(3)(a) 138
S9(3)(b) 138
S9(4) 138
Communications Act 2003... 136
Computer Misuse Act 1990 . 142
S1 142
S1(a) 142
S1(b) 142
S1(c) 142
S2 145
S17 142
S17(2) 143
S17(3) 143
S17(4) 143
S17(5) 143
S17(5)(a) 143
S17(5)(b) 144
S17(6) 144
S17(10) 143
**Coroners and Justice Act
   2009 .... 32**
S54(1) 32
S54(1)(a) 33
S54(1)(b) 34
S54(1)(c) 34, 35

S54(2) 33
S55 34
S55(3) 34
S55(4) 34
S55(5) 34
S55(6)(c) 34
Criminal Attempts Act 1981.. 26
S1 26
Criminal Appeal Act 1995 4
S8 4
Criminal Damage Act 1971 ... 82
S1 94
S1(1) 92
S5 .... 92, 93
S10 94
S10(a) 94
S10(b) 94
S10(c) 94
Criminal Justice Act 1988 47
S39 47
**Criminal Justice and
   Immigration Act 2008 ...... 142**
S76 148
S76(3) 149
S76(5) 149
S76(5A) 150
S76(6) 150
S76(6A) 150
S76(7) 150
S76(7)(a) 150
S76(7)(b) 150
S76(8) 150
Criminal Law Act 1967 149
S3 149
S3(1) 149
Computer Misuse Act 1990.. 142
S1 .... 142, 144

S1(a)	142	S5(4)	85
S1(b)	142	**Gaming Act 1845**	**75**
S1(c)	142	XVIII	75
S2	145	**Homicide Act 1957**	**35**
S2(a)	143	S2	35
S2(b)	143	S2(1)(a)	36
S17	142	S2(1)(b)	37
S17(2)	143	S2(1)(c)	37
S17(2)(a)	143	**Mental Capacity Act 2005**	**61**
S17(2)(b)	143	S2	61
S17(2)(c)	143	S2(1)	61
S17(2)(d)	143	S2(2)	61
S17(3)	143	S3(1)	61
S17(4)	143	S3(1)(a)	61
S17(5)	143	S3(1)(b)	61
S17(5)(a)	143	S3(1)(c)	61
S17(5)(b)	143	S3(1)(d)	61
S17(6)	144	**Misuse of Drugs Act 1971**	**98**
S17(10)	143	S4	98
Dangerous Dogs Act 1991	**124**	S4(1)	100
Fraud Act 2006	**83**	S4(1)(b)	104
S1	83	S4(3)	101
S2(1)	83	S4(3)(a)	102
S2(1)(a)	83	S4(3)(b)	102
S2(1)(b)	83	S4(3)(c)	92
S2(1)(c)	83	S5	98
S2(2)	84	S5(1)	98
S2(2)(a)	84	S5(2)	98
S2(2)(b)	84	S5(3)	104
S2(3)	84	S5(4)	101
S2(4)	84	S5(4)(a)	101
S2(5)	84	S5(4)(b)	101
S5	85	S28	100
S5(2)	85	S28(3)(b)(i)	100
S5(2)(a)	85	S37	37
S5(2)(b)	85	S37(1)	102
S5(3)	85	S37(3)	99

TABLE OF STATUTES

Schedule 2 parts I–III............... 99
Offences Against the Persons Act 1861 .... **49**
S18 .... 52, 53
S20 .... 50, 54
S47 .... 49, 50
Protection of Animals Act 1911.. **139**
S1 132
S1(1)(d).................................... 132
Prosecution of Offences Act 1985.. **3**
S6(1)... 3
Public Order Act 1986 .... **106**
S3 108
S3(1).. 106
S3(3).. 107
S3(4).. 110
S3(5).. 106
S4A 110
S4A(a)..................................... 110
S4A(b)..................................... 110
S4A(2)..................................... 112
S4A(3)..................................... 112
S4A(3)(a) 112
S4A(3)(b) 112
S5 113
S5(1).. 113
S5(1)(a) 113
S5(1)(b) 113
S5(3).. 113
S5(3)(a) 114
S5(3)(b) 114
S5(3)(c) 114
S6 109
S6(4).. 109
S8(a).. 107

S8(b).. 107
Psychoactive Substances Act 2016.. **98**
Road Traffic Act 1988 .... **41**
S1 41
S2 116
S2B.. 41
S3A 42
S3ZB 42
S3ZC 42
S7 43
S7A 43
S87(1)....................................... 42
S103(1)(b) 42
S143 42
S192 119
Sexual Offences Act 2003 .... **56**
S1 56
S1(1)... 56
S2 63
S2(1)... 63
S2(1)(a) 63
S2(1)(c) 63
S2(1)(d) 63
S3 65
S3(1)... 65
S3(1)(a) 65
S3(1)(b) 65
S3(1)(c) 65
S3(1)(d) 65
S4 58
S44 57
S74 .... 58, 60, 62
S75 58
S75(1)....................................... 59
S75(1)(a) 59
S75(1)(b) 59

S75(1)(c)	59	S79(8)(b)	66
S75(2)	59	S79(8)(c)	66
S75(2)(a)	59	S79(9)	57
S75(2)(b)	59	**Terrorism Act 2000**	**25**
S75(2)(c)	60	S13(1)	25
S75(2)(d)	60	**Theft Act 1968**	**70**
S75(2)(e)	60	S1(1)	70, 82
S75(2)(f)	60	S2	71
S75(3)	60	S3	72, 86
S76	58, 59	S3(1)	86
S76(1)	58	S3(2)	86
S76(1)(a)	58	S4	73
S76(1)(b)	58	S4(1)	73
S76(2)	58	S8	77
S76(2)(a)	58	S8(1)	76
S76(2)(b)	58	S9	79
S78	63	S9(1)(a)	79, 81, 82
S78(a)	64	S9(1)(b)	79, 81, 82
S78(b)	64	S9(2)	81
S79	56	S9(4)	79
S79(2)	57	S12	87, 89
S79(3)	57	S12(5)	88
S79(8)	66	S12(7)(a)	88
S79(8)(a)	66	S13	34

CHAPTER 1

How the Criminal Justice System Works

Agencies of Criminal Law
    The Police
    The CPS
    HMCTS
    Probation
    Prisons
    CCRC

The Criminal Courts
    The Magistrates' Court
    The Crown Court
    The High Court
    The Court of Appeal (Criminal Division)
    The Supreme Court / JCPC

Principles of Criminal Law
    Fair Warning
    Fair Labelling
    Autonomy
    Welfare

Agencies of Criminal Law

The Police

When most people think of the criminal law, their first thought will be the police. As the principal law enforcement arm in the UK, Home Office police forces are responsible for policing specified geographical areas. Lancashire Constabulary police Lancashire, Leicestershire Police police Leicestershire, and so on. It is noteworthy that the UK, despite being a relatively small nation still separates it's policing into even smaller localities. Specialist national forces take control of policing certain infrastructure, the British Transport Police police the railways, the Civil Nuclear Constabulary police civil nuclear sites and materials, with the MOD Police policing national defences and national infrastructure.

This often means that individual forces will have distinct and separate practices, often making domestic cross-border policing a challenge. This also serves as a confusion for individuals who operate across domestic borders. Someone living in Nottinghamshire but working in Leicestershire for example will be subjected to the same broad criminal laws, but different policing policies. This can serve to further muddy the waters of what is criminal and what is not.

Readers should make no mistake that this book focusses on the Criminal Law as it stands in England and Wales, not on policing policy. Something which is legally criminal may not always face police action. In *Blackburn*[1] it was outlined by Lord Denning M.R. that the police possess an inherent discretion as to how, when and in what circumstances they make use of their granted powers, that is a matter for the Chief Constable of a force to decide *"on the disposition of his force and the concentration of his resources on any particular crime or area."*

---

1 [1968] 2 Q.B. 118, 136

Clearly this discretion has a useful place, but for the purposes of this text we ignore it, for only when a clear understanding of the prevailing law is gained can the discretion be properly understood and appreciated.

The CPS

The Crown Prosecution Service (CPS) is the public agency responsible for the vast majority of criminal prosecutions, they also have the power to assume responsibility for private prosecutions brought by other entities under s.6(1) of the Prosecution of Offences Act 1985, which are not a recognised 'prosecuting authority', such as the RSPCA.

The CPS are headed by the Director of Public Prosecutions (DPP) and are independent of government and of the various police forces. They are made up of 14 regional teams each led by a Chief Crown Prosecutor, as well as specialist divisions including the Serious Economic, Organised Crime and International Directorate (SEOCID), the CPS Proceeds of Crime Division (CPSPOC) and the Special Crime and Counter Terrorism Division.

HMCTS

His Majesty's (HM) Courts and Tribunals Service (HMCTS) is an executive agency of the Ministry of Justice. It is responsible for the administrative functions of the Courts and Tribunals.

The Criminal Courts, require a significant amount of behind-the-scenes administration to function. Matters including listing, jury empanelment, witness attendance, the maintenance of the court estates, staffing judges, secretarial work and more are performed by a team of around 17,000 HMCTS Civil Servants under the direction of members of the Judiciary (Judges and Magistrates).

Probation

The Probation Service is a statutory criminal justice service that is responsible for the supervision of offenders released into the community.

Probation is most often engaged following a guilty plea or a guilty verdict. They will be called upon by Judges and Magistrates to write reports in regard to offenders due to be sentenced. Probation reports will help the Court pass the most appropriate sentence on the individual, the reports will often make references to an offender's: personal life; employment; physical, mental and emotional health and living circumstances.

The Courts are not bound to follow probation recommendations, but often will trust the experience of the probation officers in concluding as to sentence.

The Probation Service also engages with offenders released from custody following a period of imprisonment.

Prisons

Prisons are, of course, the institutions, be they public or private, where offenders serving custodial sentences are housed. It is worth noting that where crimes are committed in prisons, they will often not be subject to prosecution through the courts, but dealt with by way of a Prison Adjudication, which treats infractions of the law as a regulatory offence, which are disposed of at a hearing before a Prison Governor (or similar), or in some cases a District Judge (Magistrates' Courts). Serious offences are however referred, formally, to the police and the CPS with a view to Court action.

The CCRC

The Criminal Cases Review Commission are an independent body, established by s.8 of the Criminal Appeal Act 1995, with statutory powers to investigate criminal cases where there is a possibility that a person was wrongly convicted or wrongly sentenced, in circumstances where those people have lost (and exhausted) their appeals.

Between April 1997 and August 2022, the CCRC reports that they have had 774 appeals heard by the courts, of those 542 have been allowed.

The Criminal Courts

The Magistrates' Court

All criminal cases will begin in the Magistrates' Court, and the vast majority of cases will be dealt with to conclusion there. Magistrates' Courts are able to pass a maximum sentence of 12 months imprisonment on any one qualifying offence. Magistrates' Courts are presided over by either Magistrates (normally in benches of two or three) or a (Deputy) District Judge (Magistrates' Courts). Solicitors, Barristers and some members of CILEx have rights of audience before the Magistrates' Court. The Magistrates' Court does not employ formal court dress (wigs & gowns) but rather lounge suits or equivalent.

The Crown Court

The most serious of cases will be heard in the Crown Court. These cases are generally of a type which are complex in fact or law, or will result in significant sentences if the defendant is convicted. The Court sits with a Judge (responsible for decisions of law) and Jury (responsible for decision of fact), or in some cases a Judge alone. Only Barristers or Solicitor Advocates (solicitors with special training) can appear in this Court. It is generally the Crown Court that one will see depicted in English courtroom dramas. Full court dress is employed in the Crown Court, save for circumstances when the Judge grants leave owing to issues relating to the vulnerability of witnesses.

The Crown Court also hears appeals against decisions of the Magistrates' Court.

The High Court

The High Court has a very limited role in relation to criminal law, largely related to appeals on distinct points of law. Again, as with the Crown Court, only Barristers or Solicitor Advocates (solicitors with special training) can appear in this Court

The Court of Appeal (Criminal Division)

Criminal appeals are largely heard in this court. It is from the Court of Appeal that we take much of our case law. Throughout this text there are references to particular decisions of the Court of Appeal, and indeed the Supreme Court, these decisions form Judicial Precedent which is a source of law. In England and Wales, Judges interpret the law passed by parliament with the aid of previous decisions. The starting point being that of *'stare decisis'*, translated as 'let the decision stand'. Essentially, this means that unless there is reason to move away from the logic of a previous decision then that said logic should be cross-applied to the case with which the court is currently concerned (see chapter 2).

The Supreme Court & The JCPC

The highest court in England and Wales is the United Kingdom Supreme Court, this court only hears cases that have been certified to be of general public importance. For most criminal appellants, their journey of appeal will end in the Court of Appeal. Only defendants whose cases merit the attention of the Supreme Court will receive it.

The same judges (Justices) that sit on the UK Supreme Court, also make up the bench of the Judicial Committee of the Privy

Council, this is a Court which, inter alia, exercises criminal jurisdiction by acting as the final appellate court for UK overseas territories and crown dependencies, as well as those members of the commonwealth which chose to retain it. Appeal lies from a number of countries, including The Bahamas, Jamaica, and Trinidad & Tobago.

Principles of Criminal Law

In essence the Theory of Criminal Law has two broad effects; to impact the substance of the practical law (i.e. How it effects real people in real cases), and, to impact law reform – by setting strategic goals for the development of the law. The principles below are generally seen as a guiding light to the interpretation of criminal law, but readers should appreciate that the theory is separate to the law itself. It is the doctrinal law that this guide focuses on, but an awareness of the theory is of both interest and use.

Fair Warning

"Ignorantia juris non excusat."[2] It is the principle of fair warning that allows the law, in theory, to govern. The law should be known by all and therefore can legitimately bind all. Those governed by the law should be given fair warning of the contents of the law and therefore they can be justifiably held accountable by it.

Fair warning also impacts the way that law should be written. It is this theory that gave rise to the approach of 'plain English' language usage in the courts and in the legal professions. It is not enough for merely the written paper to be made available to the public, if they cannot understand the words they are given fair warning of.

---

2 "Ignorance of the Law is no excuse."

It follows therefore that the law must be clear, understandable, accessible and available. This extends to all forms of criminal law and indeed, there is much room for improvement in this regard.

Fair Labelling

The names of criminal offences are important to society, they form labels for not only the conduct which they criminalise but also the people who are convicted, and oftentimes those who are accused. It is therefore recognised that there is a requirement for the law to ensure that the names (labels) for offences accurately reflect the quality and nature of the offending behaviour they regulate.

For most of the lay public their knowledge, or *fair warning*, of criminal offences will be the names; Rape, Murder, Robbery, *et al.* This means that the fair labelling theorem is crucial in ensuring that those without advanced law degrees or legal training are able to understand which offences comprise of what behaviours, and therefore be, *Fairly Warned*.

Autonomy

Generally, autonomy is discussed as it relates to a defendant rather than anyone else. In essence autonomy is the theoretical principle by which the criminal law applies legal, as well as moral, blameworthiness. A Defendant *chooses* to pursue a course of conduct, or indeed chooses not to pursue a course of conduct, therefore, if that conduct, or that failure is criminal the Defendant *chooses* to commit crime, and therefore can be blamed for his choice.

This principle also protects defendants, in practice through defences such as duress or insanity – where the Defendant is compelled to act either through threat or indeed a recognised medical condition – they will not be blamed.

Welfare

Generally seen as the principle which transcends the criminal law, just as unlawful autonomous actions come with blame and criminalisation, lawful autonomous actions come with protection. The criminal law fundamentally is there to protect society – the welfare principle achieves this by recognising the need for minimum criminalisation, so that autonomy can be exercised wherever possible, but the welfare of society can be protected.

CHAPTER 2

Defining Crime

Sources of Criminal Law
   Statutory Offences
   Common Law Offences

Elements of an Offence
   Actus Reus
   Causation
   Mens Rea
   Specific and Basic intent crimes
   Strict Liability
   The Absence of a Defence
   Conduct & Result Crimes

Note on Attempted Offences

Sources of Criminal Law

Broadly speaking, the Criminal Law of England and Wales can be categorised into two distinct sources. The distinction between the two is discussed in appropriate detail below. In essence, some offences exist because of past court cases, and some because of an express and positive act of the legislature (i.e., Parliament).

Statutory Offences

Offences of Statute, or Legislative Offences are crimes which are created by virtue of an enactment. This is a process by which Parliament debates and passes certain laws which reflect contemporary society. These offences often last, as you will see in the 'non-fatal offences against the person' chapter of this book, that even now in 2023 serious 'assaults' are charged by way of an enactment from 1861.[3]

Statutory offences are often drafted in a way which purports to be clear and unambiguous, though this is not always the case. It is statutory offences, however, which the public often find easiest to understand when reading law. The definitions of legislative offences are often self-contained within a statute itself, sometimes even a single section – this means they can often be read simply and quickly. Statutory offences generally employ the use of plain English.

Common Law Offences

Offences at Common Law come into being by way of the Doctrine of Judicial Precedent and the concept of *stare decisis*, essentially a position in English and Welsh law which maintains that once a decision has been made, normally by a senior court,

---

[3] Offences Against the Person Act 1861

that decision should stand, and be followed in other cases, unless there is a good reason to do otherwise.

Because of this, offences at common law are often more difficult for the layman to understand, often requiring detailed knowledge of several leading cases in order to garner an understanding of the offence in all its forms. These leading cases can be centuries old, so the language is often archaic, with Latin maxims being commonplace.

Take for example the definition of Murder;

"Murder is when a man of sound memory and of the age of discretion, unlawfully killeth within any county of the realm any reasonable creature in rerum natura under the king's peace, with malice aforethought, either expressed by the party or implied by law..."[4]

It is clear that the language, still good in law, used to define the common law offence of Murder is both outdated and inaccessible to the layman. This flies in the face of the rule of law, which acknowledges that the law should be able to be understood and be accessible. The use of archaic terminology exiles those not legally educated to an intellectual existence based on guesswork and supposition.

Elements of an Offence

An offence in law, be it statutory or common, is generally considered to be a combination of an action or inaction with a criminal state of mind. There are exceptions to this rule, but if readers approach most offences using this formula, then they will not stray too far from the correct path.

See the formula, represented mathematically below.

Actus Reus + Mens Rea + the absence of a defence = criminal liability

---

[4] Edward Coke, *Coke's Institutes* (1628, Part III, Chapter 7, page 47)

Actus Reus

Latin for Guilty Act. Though senior jurists have argued for the abandonment of the Latin translations, they remain in common occurrence. Helpfully in *Miller*[5], Lord Diplock mused that;

> *"it would I think be conducive to clarity of analysis of the ingredients of a crime that is created by statute, as are the great majority of criminal offences today, if we were to avoid bad Latin and instead to think and speak ... about the conduct of the accused and his state of mind at the time of that conduct, instead of speaking of actus reus and mens rea."*

It becomes clear therefore, when discussing *actus reus* – the guilty act, those seeking to understand it as a facet of law, should consider the actions, and indeed the inactions, of a defendant and whether those correlate to the elements of the particular offence under consideration.

Generally, *actus reus* will take the form of one of four circumstances;

- A positive action by the defendant
- Inaction (an omission) by a defendant when they are required to act in law
- The manifestation of a specific result, or,
- The existence of a state of affairs

Positive actions by the defendant, are the simplest of the circumstances, it is the punch, the kick, the taking, or the pulling of a trigger – it's the 'doing thing' described verbally.

Inaction, often referred to in law as 'omissions', are the failure by a defendant to actively undertake a positive action, they generally carry no criminal consequences. A person, unconnected in law to the drowning child, bears no criminal liability if when able to save the child they choose not to do so.

---

5 [1983] 2 AC 161

The culpable element arises when the person is under a duty to act. A duty is generally seen to arise in five circumstances, which can (and do) intersect.

- Voluntary Assumption of Responsibility
- Statutory duties
- Contractual Duties
- Duties by special relationships, and/or,
- The duty to avert a danger of one's own making.

VOLUNTARY ASSUMPTION

To explain voluntary assumption, we turn to *Nicholls*[6] wherein a grandmother took their grandchild in and expressly accepted that she would care for the child. The child was neglected and died. The grandmother was convicted of manslaughter, because she had voluntarily accepted the responsibility for her grandchild, and therefore was under a duty to act – she failed to act and therefore in that circumstance the voluntary assumption of responsibility, by the grandmother, to act gave rise to criminal liability.

The assumption, however, need not be expressed, it may be implied. In *Instan*[7] the defendant was a niece of an infirm aunt – only the defendant was aware of the aunt's ill health. The defendant failed (omitted) to care for the aunt or, indeed, summon medical assistance. On hearing the defendant's appeal Lord Coleridge CJ, held that, although moral obligations will not always result in the implication of a legal duty, there is an argument that legal duties follow from moral obligations. The fact that the defendant was being maintained by the aunt's money, and in the aunt's home, meant, in the Court's view, that the defendant niece was under a duty to secure the aunt's health by way of nutrition and medical assistance, *"so much as was necessary"*.

---

6 (1874) 13 Cox CC 75
7 [1893] 1 QB 450

Statutory Duties

On occasion people, or classes of people, will be made subject to duties proscribed by enactment. By way of an example s.172[8] places a duty upon the registered keeper of a motor vehicle to provide information as to the identity of the driver when requested to do so by the chief officer of police, where the driver is alleged to be guilty of an offence under the same enactment. A failure to discharge this statutory duty, would result in the imposition of criminal liability.

Contractual Duties

Employment (and other) contracts will often create duties to which the parties to the contract will be bound. These clauses often surround matters of health and safety. The relationship between contract law and the criminal law is one of distance. Civil law being regulated to a lower standard of proof, and criminal law having much further reaching consequences. That being said, in relation to omissions the criminal law relies on contracts in certain circumstances to impute a duty onto a defendant where one would not, but for the contract, exist. In *Pittwood*[9], the leading caselaw in relation to contractual duties, the defendant was the operator of a railway crossing before the days of motorisation. Under his contract of employment, he was required to shut the gate of the crossing whenever a train was passing through. The defendant on one occasion went on his lunch break and failed to lower the crossing gate for the duration of his absence. During this absence, a cart passed over the crossing and the driver was killed. The court held that the driver was under a duty to act in line with his contract, and his failure in this regard could therefore result in criminal culpability as a failure to act.

---

8 Road Traffic Act 1988
9 (1902) 19 TLR 37

DUTIES BY SPECIAL RELATIONSHIPS

As humans in existence, we do not operate in a vacuum, it follows therefore that we will have a connection, to greater or lesser extents, with those that surround us. This is the premise of duties which arise because of 'special' relationships. The distinction between the connections between human beings as a species and the connection to which the law, in this regard, refers is the word 'special'. This means that the connection, or relationship, that exists between a potential defendant and the relevant injured party, must be one that is so closely connected that an action, or inaction, in breach of it must be considered criminal.

Take for example, *Gibbins*[10], wherein the two defendants lived with the first defendant's child whom they omitted to feed, causing her death. Gibbins, the first defendant, as the child's father was held by the court to have a 'special relationship' with the child, his child, and so was decided to be criminally culpable for his daughter's death.

Further, in *Smith*[11] and *Hood*[12] the court suggest that, in certain circumstances, a spouse will have a duty towards their significant other, though clearly, the duty will likely not be as onerous as that which exists between parent and child.

The key consideration it seems however, does not emanate from the labels of the relationship, mother/son, husband/wife, but from the specifics and subjective elements of the relationship itself, in essence the 'closeness' of the relationship.

It may be therefore that an estranged couple still technically married would not be subject to a relevant duty, whereas very close friends may well be.

---

10 *Gibbins and Proctor* (1918) 12 Cr App R 134
11 [1979] Crim LR 251
12 [2004] 1 Cr App R (S) 73

Aversion of a danger of one's own making

'You broke it – you fix it'. If a person creates a danger, they must, themselves, take reasonable steps to rectify the danger. Take an oil spillage on a busy motorway, once the driver knew that he had leaked the oil, he would have created a danger to other traffic. He would then be under a duty to take reasonable steps to rectify it. The question then becomes what is reasonable? It would, clearly, be reasonable for the driver to pull over, switch his hazards on and call the relevant authorities, it would not be reasonable for the driver to stand in the middle of the carriageway jumping up and down to warn oncoming traffic.

In *Miller*[13] the Defendant accidentally lit fire to a mattress, by falling asleep with a lit cigarette, upon realising the fire he had set, rather than calling the fire brigade he went into an adjoining room and went back to sleep. The fire caused significant damage. The Court of Appeal considered the inaction, upon realising the blaze, constituted a breach of his 'duty to avert', and that he could therefore be held culpable for the arson.

Causation

Some crimes require the defendant, as part of the *actus reus* requirements to 'cause' a particular thing to happen. To be convicted of an assault occasioning actual bodily harm for example, the defendant must cause some harm to a victim.

Causation in law comprises of two elements, both of which must be satisfied in order for a defendant to be said to have 'caused' something. These are 'factual' and 'legal' causation.

Factual Causation

This is the broad scope of causation, to be the factual cause of a result the result must be said to have not occurred, *but for* the defendant's conduct. For example, 'but for the gunshot wound,

---

13 [1983] 2 AC 161

the victim would not have died'. In *White*[14] the defendant placed poison in his mother's night-time drink, his mother was found dead the following morning. However, medical evidence showed that she had in fact died as a result of heart failure, not poisoning. As a result, therefore the son could not be convicted of Murder as he was not the factual cause of his mother's death.

In *Mitchell*[15] the court applied the but for test in respect of a domino-like push. The defendant (D) was in a queue and became impatient, he pushed the person in front of him (A), who then fell into the person in front of them (B). B died as a result of her injuries. In this case the test for factual causation, the but for test, can be simply applied.

But for D pushing A, A would not have fallen into B, and but for A falling into B then B would not have died. Therefore, D is the factual cause of B's death.

It is clear that on its own, factual causation would leave the scope of causation in law far too wide. Encompassing far too many factors, in the above example, but for the first post office being closed, B would not have been forced to use the other, so it is the fault of the first office manager, or, but for B needing to post a letter, she wouldn't have died, so is it her own fault, or the fault of the company to whom she was sending the letter, but for B's parents giving birth B would not have existed in the first place, this list goes on.

Readers may wish to consider the writings from Lord Hughes, in the decision of the Supreme Court, in the case of *Hughes*[16] (unrelated), for further discussion of the absurdity of the operation of factual causation in isolation.

This is why, concurrently to factual causation, a defendant must also be the legal cause of the result.

---

14 [1910] 2 KB 124
15 [1983] QB 741
16 [2013] UKSC 56

Legal Causation

Legal causation is what narrows the field, it is the point by which we rate the 'blameworthiness' of the cause. For something to be the legal cause of a result it must be both the operating and substantial cause of the result, and it must not be negated by a new intervening act.

In *Smith*[17] the Courts-Martial Appeal Court established that, in addition to satisfying the requirements of factual causation, and in order to be the 'cause in law' of a prohibited result, the defendants' action(s) must be the "operating and substantial" cause of the result. This does not mean that the defendants' actions must be the only cause, or indeed, the main cause. It does mean however, that once a defendant's action is adjudged to be merely trivial, or trifling, the defendant will be absolved of the imputation of the label of the 'legal cause'.

Further to the rule in *Smith* a defendant's actions will not be the legal cause of a result if there is a *novus actus interveniens* (a new intervening act), which, in essence, breaks the link between the defendant's initial blameworthy conduct and the result suffered by the victim, this link is often referred to as the 'chain of causation'. Generally, intervening acts take one of three forms; an act of the victim, an act of a third party, and acts of God. To break the chain of causation the potential intervening act must go beyond something which merely aggravates the initial act, or contributes to an increase in severity, it must take a form which is so overwhelming that the initial actions of the defendant become something which could only be considered a co-incidental occurrence, and not, a, true, legal cause.

Acts of the victim – in *Blaue*[18] the victim was attacked by the defendant and was taken to hospital where she was advised by doctors that she needed a blood transfusion. Being a Jehovah's

---

17 (Thomas Joseph) [1959] 2 QB 35
18 *(Kenneth Joseph)* [1975] 3 All ER 446

Witness, the victim refused and died. Lawton LJ, giving judgment of the Court of Appeal, held that; *"The fact that the victim refused to stop this end coming about did not break the causal connection between the act and death."* It follows that any reasonable act of the victim cannot be said to be a valid new intervening act, and that, for the victim to be a new intervening act their action must be wholly unreasonable in the circumstances. In *Roberts*[19] the victim accepted an offer of transport from the Defendant, during the drive, the defendant began to make unwanted sexual advances, on repeated occasions. The victim, in order to escape, jumped out of the moving car, suffering actual bodily harm. The Court held that the victims' actions were a *"natural result"* of the defendants' actions, in essence, that they were reasonable. Only if the victim does an act which is so *"daft, ... or so unexpected, not ... that this particular assailant did not actually foresee it but that no reasonable man could be expected to foresee it..."* that their act will break the chain of causation and therefore absolve the defendant of culpability for the result.

Acts of third parties – a defendant, acting voluntarily, will generally be the legal cause of the result if it was the last 'input' in the lead up to it. But, notably when a third party intervenes, their actions must be closely examined. If the *type* of risk and harm was foreseeable, for example harm arising out of negligent medical intervention, or a botched police response, then the chain of causation will likely not be broken.

By way of an example, in *Pagett*[20] the defendant was using a 16-year-old girl as a human shield during a stand-off with armed police officers. Following the defendant firing at the police, the police marksmen, on instinct, returned fire, causing the 16-year-old girl to suffer gunshot wounds and, resultantly, death. In such a case the Jury could properly apply the law

---

19 (1972) 56 Cr. App. R. 95
20 *(Keith David)* (1983) 76 Cr. App. R. 279

on causation by saying that, it is clearly foreseeable that upon shooting at armed police officers, you may expect to receive fire back, and by using a person as a shield, it is foreseeable that they might get injured (the very nature of a shield), hence the police shooting the girl, cannot be said to be a true *novus actus interveniens*, it must be considered a *"natural result"* of the defendant's actions, and hence not a break in the chain of causation.

Acts of God – in *Southern Water Authority v Pegrum*[21] the court held that to break the chain of causation, an Act of God, sometimes termed an 'exceptional natural event' must be *"of so powerful a nature that the conduct of the defendant was not a cause at all but was merely a part of the surrounding circumstances."* This assessment can be taken as somewhat reflective of the general position in relation to new intervening acts, but especially so in terms of Acts of God – the High Court in *Pegrum* confirms that only the operation of natural forces so unpredictable can eradicate the defendant's culpability. If the forces are so predictable, such as the heavy rainfall in *Pegrum*, the defendant will retain criminal liability.

The traditional example, as given in Blackstone's Criminal Practice 2023, demonstrates such an occurrence well, the editors state, that;

> *"If D attacks V and leaves V slowly dying of the injuries, the chain of causation **may** be broken if V is ultimately killed by a lightning bolt or a falling tree, rather than by the original injuries. In contrast, routine hazards, such as seasonal rain or cold winter nights, would not have such an effect."* (Emphasis added)

Readers should note that whilst there is a significant body of law that governs legal causation, it remains a question of fact for the Jury to decide.

---

21 [1989] Crim LR 442

Mens Rea

Mens Rea is read to mean 'guilty mind'. It is the requirement that makes the difference between an innocent taking of a biscuit from Grandma's tin and the dishonest theft of biscuits from the McVitie's warehouse (other biscuit brands available).

Offences generally require the defendant to have a guilty mind, in addition to, and at the same time as, they commit the guilty act. The *actus reus* and the *mens rea* must be coincidental, they must occur together, even if only for a moment, but they must run in parallel at some stage for many offences to be satisfied.

There are differing levels of *mens rea*, they are summarised below:

Direct Intent – this applies to crimes where only if the defendant's aim and purpose was to commit the guilty act, can the defendant be said to have committed the full offence. Murder is a specific intent crime, which will be considered later in this text. The defendant must act with the aim and purpose to kill or cause really serious harm, without that mental state, that guilty mind, they can be said to have killed, but cannot be said to have murdered.

Oblique Intent – this will be considered in the section of this text which deals with Murder.

Recklessness – this applies to crimes where a defendant can be seen to have chosen to take a risk that cannot be justified. In *Cunningham*[22] the Defendant removed a gas meter from the wall, not in the usual way, in order to steal the money from inside. Due to the damage, which he caused by improperly removing the meter, gas escaped and spread to living quarters, where an occupant inhaled the gas and suffered harm. The Court of Appeal, allowing the Defendant's appeal against conviction,

---

22 [1957] 2 QB 396

quashed the conviction – as the Defendant did not appreciate that a risk of harm was present when he broke the gas meter. In short, he did not see the risk, and choose to take it.

In 1982 the Court considered the case of *Caldwell*[23], which sought to change the standard of recklessness. This text will not consider *Caldwell* in any great detail as in 2004, the House of Lords considered the case of G[24] which confirmed that *Cunningham* recklessness is to be considered the authoritative position in relation to all offences requiring recklessness. Stating, *inter alia*, that Caldwell Recklessness is *"neither moral nor just"*.

Negligence – there is some debate as to whether negligence should be considered a type of Mens Rea, indeed this author considered that it should not be. But nevertheless, it will be addressed in the part of this text dealing with Gross Negligence Manslaughter.

Knowledge – some crimes only require knowledge, such as the need to know that one is in possession of something (see discussion on simple possession), this is a very low bar so is generally only used (as a sole *mens rea* requirement) for minor offences.

> *Specific and Basic intent crimes*
>
> **Basic Intent Crimes** – this applies to crimes where <u>either</u> intention or recklessness will satisfy the requirement for the guilty mind.
>
> **Specific Intent Crimes** – this applies to crimes where <u>only</u> intent will satisfy the requirement for the guilty mind.
>
> Readers should refer back to this chapter when reading the offences below. For most offences, it has been indicated

---

23 [1982] AC 341
24 [2004] 1 AC 1034

> whether a crime is one of basic or specific intent, or are otherwise formed, as the case may be from time to time. For this reason, unless the *mens rea* is more complex than either a basic or specific intent crime, then it will not be discussed save for identifying whether the specific offence is one of basic or specific intention.

Strict Liability

As outlined, generally offences will require a guilty mind, a *mens rea* in order to be completed. There are exceptions to that principle, those exceptions are termed as *offences of strict liability*. In essence, these are the offences where even if the defendant was acting entirely innocently, and with the best of intentions, they will remain liable.

Take for example, a car crossing the threshold of a red traffic light to clear a way for an ambulance travelling on blue lights and sirens. Whilst, morally, the defendant can be said to have done the correct thing – legally they will still commit an offence. Even if their action was completely safe, and morally justified.

In *Pwr v DPP*[25] the Supreme Court were considering the offence relating to the wearing of uniforms of proscribed organisations[26]. Their lordships established that in circumstances where the language of a statutory offence does not prescribe a *mens rea* element, the presumption of the need for *mens rea* can be adequately rebutted.

The Absence of a Defence

Defences will be considered later in this text, either alongside relevant offences or in the 'General Defences' chapter. But they are worth a mention at this stage. It will suffice to outline

---

25 [2022] 1 WLR 789
26 Terrorism Act 2000, s.13(1)

that where a defendant has committed the offence in law, i.e., all elements of Actus Reus and Mens Rea have been satisfied they will stand convicted of the offence, unless they can prove that they have an excuse why they should not. This is called a defence. Defences take many forms, the most well-known being that of Self-Defence.

Conduct & Result Crimes

Conduct Crimes – these are crimes which criminalise conduct alone. It is enough that the mere behaviour was committed with the relevant intention, there does not have to be any consequences of the behaviour at all.

Result Crimes – these are crimes that criminalise the consequences of certain behaviour. They require a result to a defendants conduct. Without the result, there will be no offence.

Note on Attempted Offences

s.1 Criminal Attempts Act 1981, outlines that where an individual commits an act which is more than merely preparatory to the commission of a relevant offence (most serious offences), that person will be guilty of attempting to commit the offence, and will be liable for a sentence in line with the relevant full offence.

I suggest later in this text some further reading in respect of attempted offences. I would point my readers to Mark Thomas' text, he provides an excellent explanation of the law on attempts.

CHAPTER 3

Fatal Offences Against the Person

Murder

Voluntary Manslaughter
    Loss of Control
    Diminished Responsibility

Involuntary Manslaughter
    Constructive (Unlawful Act Manslaughter)
    Gross Negligence Manslaughter

Final Chapter Notes

Murder

Murder is an offence of Common Law, meaning that it has been shaped and moulded over the centuries through the doctrine of judicial precedent. The formal definition of Murder is taken from a book written by Sir Edward Coke (1552 – 1634), a former Attorney General and Judge who had personally tried the trial arising from the Gunpowder Plot of 1605. His works have been hugely influential throughout the common law world.

Coke defines Murder as the *'Unlawful killing of a reasonable creature in rerum natura under the King's peace, with malice aforethought, either expressed by the party or implied by the law'*.[27]

In the modern day, this language is often seen as outdated. It can be explained by breaking the offence of Murder into five distinct elements.

- Unlawfulness
- Killing
- Reasonable Creature
- Under the King's peace
- With Intention

UNLAWFULNESS

A person who is subject to the laws and usages of the English realm can kill another person, provided that killing is lawful. A killing will be lawful, for example, where deadly force is used in self-defence, or defence of another. For example, in *Pagett*[28], armed police officers shot a person who was being used as a human shield, whilst the aggressor was shooting at the officers, as the officers were acting in 'lawful self-defence through a reasonable use of force.' A killing of this nature would be considered to be lawful in its nature, even though an innocent was killed, the action was in self-defence.

---

27 *Coke's Institutes*, 3 Co Inst 47
28 (1983) 76 Cr App R 279

Lawfulness is often closely examined in the context of hospital treatment. The law makes a distinction between the lawful withdrawal of treatment and the positive infliction of death. In *Airedale NHS Trust v Bland*[29] the Court of Appeal confirmed that where treatment is legitimately withdrawn in line with a reasonable body of medical opinion such a situation should not be equated with the unlawful actions as seen in cases such as *Inglis*[30] wherein Lord Judge CJ, outlined that killings of 'mercy' remain unlawful in the absence of some partial or full defence. Further, in *R (Nicklinson) v Ministry of Justice*[31] the Court considered the question of, consensual, assisted suicide. Nicklinson argued that there were human rights considerations which should allow for those wishing to end their life to seek assistance to do so. The High Court formed the view, that, in law, no such assistance could be given without amounting to the offence of Murder. Nicklinson appealed to the Court of Appeal[32], and then to the Supreme Court[33] both of which confirmed the decision of the High Court that, *inter alia*, the need to protect vulnerable individuals from being pressured into suicide outweighs the interference by the state in the right to respect for the private life of those wishing to be assisted to die.

KILLING

The element of 'killing' requires a defendant to have 'caused' a death. This is taken to mean that to satisfy the 'killing' element of the offence a defendant must be both the factual and legal cause of the victim's death. Murder is a result crime, so it is clear that a death must result.

---

29 [1983] AC 789
30 [2010] EWCA Crim 2637
31 [2012] EWHC 2381 (Admin)
32 [2013] EWCA Civ 961
33 [2015] AC 657

Reasonable Creature

Murder required the killing to be of a 'reasonable creature in *rerum natura*', in essence, it must be a human being, of its own existence.

Poulton[34] confirms that only when a baby is born alive, and has an existence independent of its mother, can it be considered to be a human being. It is therefore impossible to Murder an unborn child, though there are other offences which cover this scenario.

Interestingly, a personality who has an existence biologically-dependant on another can be considered a person. In *Re A (Children) (Conjoined twins: surgical separation)*[35] the Court confirmed that a conjoined twin, who was totally biologically-dependant on its twin for a supply of oxygenated blood was to be considered a reasonable creature in being. It seems therefore that the Court's distinction is in relation to the birthing process, and an existence, 'within the world' as opposed to an existence 'within the body'.

King's / Queen's Peace

This is generally a matter of more historical importance than contemporary significance. It should not concern readers particularly, other than to note that this element speaks to the status of the victim, not the status of the killer. As to whether they are subject to the Monarch's Peace. In *Adebelajo*[36] the Defendant, who had led the joint enterprise that killed Fusilier Lee Rigby in 2013, presented an argument to the Court that he was at war with the late Queen Elizabeth II, and therefore was not under the Queen's peace.

The Criminal Division of the Court of Appeal held, with exceptional clarity, that; *"The argument was completely hopeless.*

---

34 (1832) 5 C&P 329
35 [2001] 4 All ER 961
36 [2014] EWCA Crim 2779

We have set out at some length why it was hopeless; it should never have been advanced. We dismiss this ground of appeal as entirely misconceived."[37]

WITH INTENTION

Murder is a specific intent crime, *"...malice aforethought"* can be taken to mean intention. A distinction is then made between intention which is *"expressed"* and that which is *"implied"*. Express intention relates to an intention to kill, whereas implied intention relates to an intention to cause GBH.

Both express, and implied intention can be direct, or oblique.

Oblique intention can be satisfied by virtue of a two-stage test, emanating from the case of *Woolin*[38]. A jury are entitled to find intention where; firstly, the result was virtually certain to materialise as a result of the defendant's conduct, and; secondly, where the defendant appreciated that was the case.

By way of an example, say a mechanic rigs the brake cables on her girlfriend's car to snap at 70mph after discovering an affair, with the aim that her car gets damaged in a crash. It is clear that the mechanic would have the direct intention to cause property damage. But it is also virtually certain that really serious bodily injury, to at least the driver, will occur if the car's brakes become inoperable at 70mph, and the mechanic would have appreciated this; thus, the mechanic's jury at any subsequent trial, may find that the mechanic had an oblique intention to cause really serious bodily injury.

Oblique intention is a complex concept and a detailed explanation of it falls outside the scope of this Straightforward Guide, but my recommendations for further reading provide a fuller commentary on this concept.

---

37   Ibid, at [33], per Lord Thomas CJ.
38   [1999] AC 82

Voluntary Manslaughter

Voluntary Manslaughter is not an offence in its own right, but instead, the operation, of one of two partial defences. Partial defences, unlike complete defences do not result in an acquittal but in a reduction of the offence label. In this case, the operation of either of the partial defences of Loss of Control, or, Diminished Responsibility, will reduce a conviction of what would otherwise have been Murder, to the offence label of Manslaughter.

Both Loss of Control and Diminished Responsibility are statutory defences, and, in the case of Loss of Control, replaced the old common-law defence of provocation.

Loss of Control

The Coroners and Justice Act 2009 came into force in 2010 and modernised the law in relation to what used to be considered provocation. It is noteworthy to readers of this text that the Court of Appeal have been explicit in asserting that it;

> "...should rarely be necessary to look at cases decided under the old law of provocation. When it is necessary, the cases must be considered in the light of the fact that the defence of loss of control is a defence different to provocation and is fully encompassed within the statutory provisions."[39]

Under s.54(1) of the 2009 Act, a person is not to be convicted of Murder if;

    a. D's acts and omissions in doing or being a party to the killing resulted from D's loss of self-control,
    b. the loss of self-control had a qualifying trigger, and

---

[39] Gurpinar [2015] 1 Cr App R 31 (464)

c. a person of D's sex and age, with a normal degree of tolerance and self-restraint and in the circumstances of D, might have reacted in the same or in a similar way to D.

Readers will note, the use of the word *"and"* in paragraph b, means that in order to access the partial defence, a defendant must satisfy all of the elements laid down within paragraphs a-c.

s.54(1)(a) – Killing due to D's Loss of Self Control

Under s.54(2) the loss of control need not be sudden. Loss of Control is generally0 understood to take its ordinary meaning, but case law provides some useful guidance. In *Jewell (Darren)*[40], Rafferty LJ, referencing the 13th Edition of Smith & Hogan's Criminal Law (see further reading list), outlined that a Loss of Control under s.54(1)(a) will involve the *"loss of the Defendant's ability to act in accordance with considered judgment or a loss of normal powers of reasoning"*.

It is clear therefore that any decision or calculation to peruse a course of conduct amounting to revenge, will not fall within the remit of s.54(1)(a). In *Clinton*[41] Lord Judge CJ, approved a judicial direction which explained that *"a considered act of revenge, whether performed calmly or in anger, is not a loss of self-control"*[42]

Indeed, any calculated decisions will not amount to a loss of control. In *Nixon*[43] the Court held that; where a defendant *"may well have lost his temper and reacted aggressively to what may well have been violence from the deceased... [would be] a long way from evidence that he had lost his self-control"*[44].

---

40 [2014] EWCA Crim 414
41 [2013] QB 1
42 Ibid, at [128]
43 [2020] EWCA Crim 336
44 Ibid, at para.8(iv)

s.54(1)(b) – Qualifying Triggers

The loss of self-control under s.54(1)(a) must arise as a result of a qualifying trigger, per, s.54(1)(b) of the 2009 Act, said triggers are outlined by virtue of s.55(3-5) of the 2009 Act as follows;

> s.55(3) – "if D's loss of self-control was attributable to D's fear of serious violence from V against D or another identified person."
> s.55(4) – "This subsection applies if D's loss of self-control was attributable to a thing or things done or said (or both) which (a) constituted circumstances of an extremely grave character, and (b) caused D to have a justifiable sense of being seriously wronged."
> s.55(5) – "This subsection applies if D's loss of self-control was attributable to a combination of the matters mentioned in subsections (3) and (4)"

It is clear therefore that the new triggers under s.55 seek to restrict the possibility of defences arising because a defendant 'just saw red and snapped' – there now needs to be a qualified justification (trigger) for the loss of control. Without this, a defendant who would have previously had access to the defence of provocation, will no longer be able to avail himself of any protection under the modern law resulting from the assent of the 2009 Act.

Interestingly, s.55(6)(c), expressly excludes sexual infidelity as a 'thing said or done', this presumably is done to limit occurrences of the use of this partial defence in such circumstances, as infidelity is in such rife supply in modern day society that what once was met with significant disapproval by the common law, may now fail to raise even an eyebrow.

Again, the three triggers are a complex concept, a fuller discussion of which falls outside the scope of this text, readers wishing to consider these in further detail should consult further recommended texts.

s.54(1)(c) – Objective test, in subjective circumstances

This provision requires the Court to consider whether an ordinary person, would, when placed in the Defendant's circumstances have reacted in either the same, or a similar, way.

This, essentially, means that where a Defendant has a 'hot temper' or is generally one to act on impulse those factors will be excluded. It is not a defence to be 'hot-headed' but only to truly lose control, by the standards of an ordinary person in specific circumstances.

In *Wilcocks*[45] the Court of Appeal approved an explanation by example in the following terms;

> "... a personality disorder which made him unusually likely to become angry and aggressive at the slightest provocation, ... could not assist him in relation to loss of control. But if you thought that a personality disorder had caused him to attempt suicide, then you would have been entitled to take into account as one of his circumstances the effect on him of being taunted that he should have killed himself."

It is clear therefore that the test under s.54(1)(c) serves to restrict the defence becoming available to individuals except in the most exceptional of circumstance.

Diminished Responsibility

Diminished Responsibility is another partial statutory defence to Murder. Like Loss of Control, the successful operation of the defence will reduce, what would otherwise be a conviction of Murder, to one of Manslaughter.

It is important not to confuse the partial defence of Diminished Responsibility with the full defence of Insanity.

This partial defence is outlined in the Homicide Act 1957, s.2 (as amended);

---

45 [2017] 1 Cr App R 23

> a. A person ('D') who kills or is a party to the killing of another is not to be convicted of murder if D was suffering from an abnormality of mental functioning which —
>   a. arose from a recognised medical condition,
>   b. substantially impaired D's ability to do one or more of the things mentioned in subsection (1A), and
>   c. provides an explanation for D's acts and omissions in doing or being a party to the killing.

ABNORMALITY OF MENTAL FUNCTIONING

Originally referred to as an 'abnormality of mind' this refers to the functioning of the mind "in all its aspects"[46]. This element of the defence purposely avoids the psychological theory previously considered under the old language. It enables juries to focus on the 'normalness' of a defendant's mental processes, i.e. How 'normally' or 'abnormally' does a defendant process thought.

S.2(1)(A) – RECOGNISED MEDICAL CONDITION

The abnormality of mental functioning must arise, because of a recognised medical condition.

There is no definitive list of conditions which satisfy this element of the defence, reference is often made to various psychiatric and medical manuals but the Courts have made it clear that not all medically recognised conditions will give access to the defence. In *Dowds*[47] the Court of Appeal held that a recognised medical condition is; *"a necessary, but not always sufficient, condition to raise the issue of diminished responsibility"*. The Court goes on to note that conditions arising from voluntary intoxication, will not give rise to the defence, nor, as the Court observed in *Lindo*[48] would conditions arising out of voluntary drug taking.

---

46 *Byrne* [1960] 2 QB 396, (Per Lord Parker CJ, at 403)
47 [2012] 1 Cr App R 34 (455)
48 [2016] EWCA Crim 1940

s.2(1)(B) – Substantial Impairment

The Act requires that the abnormality of mental functioning, which arose from a recognised medical condition, *impairs* a defendant's ability to do three things, outlined in s.2(1A).

> (1A) Those things are —
> (a) to understand the nature of D's conduct;
> (b) to form a rational judgment;
> (c) to exercise self-control.

In *Golds*[49] the Supreme Court held that the word 'substantial' did not take it's ordinary meaning of 'something of substance' but instead should be read as being equivalent to 'something important or weighty'. Lord Hughes provided a summary of the need for the higher bar in cases of Diminished Responsibility. He said that; "the reduction to the lesser offence to be occasioned where there is a weighty reason for it and not merely a reason which just passes the trivial."[50]

s.2(1)(C) – Providing an Explanation

There is no requirement for the abnormality of mental functioning to be the sole cause of the killing. But it must explain why the defendant did, or did not do, the relevant act that caused death.

s.2(1B) outlines that *"For the purposes of subsection (1)(c), an abnormality of mental functioning provides an explanation for D's conduct if it causes, or is a significant contributory factor in causing, D to carry out that conduct."*

So, in essence, as long as the abnormality of mental functioning is, *at least*, a significant factor in causing the defendant to kill. It will satisfy the requirement under s.2(1)(c).

---

49 [2017] 1 Cr App R 18
50 Ibid, at [36]

Involuntary Manslaughter

Involuntary Manslaughter is the type of manslaughter that most people are somewhat aware of. In essence, voluntary manslaughter, as discussed above, would otherwise satisfy the test for Murder, there would have been an intention to kill.

Involuntary Manslaughter however deals with situations where there was no intention to kill. There are three types of Involuntary Manslaughters, all are offences in their own right. They are; Constructive Manslaughter, Gross Negligence Manslaughter, and Corporate Manslaughter. The former two will be discussed in this text, the latter will not.

Constructive (Unlawful Act Manslaughter)

Constructive Manslaughter, often referred to as Unlawful Act Manslaughter, requires a defendant to commit an unlawful (criminal) act which is dangerous, and results in death.

UNLAWFUL ACT

The defendant's conduct, which caused (see discussion on factual and legal causation in Chapter 2) death, must be a criminal offence, independently of the result of death. Generally, the unlawful act will be some form of offence against the person (see chapter 4), but could equally be an offence against property, such as Arson or indeed something that had a high chance of causing harm. The editors of Blackstones' Criminal Practice give an example from the case of *Nica*[51] where *"the unlawful act being the offence of facilitating a breach or attempted breach of immigration law in circumstances known to D (concealment in an air-tight container lorry) objectively likely to cause some harm."*[52] But it is of note that a defendant must commit the conduct which

---

51 [2021] EWCA Crim 1790
52 Blackstones Criminal Practice 2023 (OUP, London) at B1.57

causes the death, so offences such as Affray will not satisfy the requirement, as exemplified in the case of *Carey*[53].

A defendant, when committing the unlawful act, must have the *mens rea* for the unlawful act itself. In *Lamb*[54] the Defendant pointed a loaded revolver at his friend and pulled the trigger, the friend died. The Defendant's conviction for constructive manslaughter was quashed as he did not have the *mens rea* of the unlawful act, the shooting which required intention or recklessness – he honestly believed there were no bullets in the gun capable of being fired, nor did he intend to frighten his friend. He was, tragically, only joking.

DANGEROUSNESS

In *Church*[55], Edmund Davis J, outlined that; *"... the unlawful act must be such as all sober and reasonable people would inevitably recognise must subject the other person to, at least, the risk of some harm resulting therefrom, albeit not serious harm."*[56]

Clearly therefore the unlawful action must be such that the reasonable observer would consider to pose the risk that 'some harm' (see discussion of ABH in chapter 4) would result from the Defendant's conduct. The 'some harm' must be physical harm and not emotional harm.

Gross Negligence Manslaughter

In civil law (the law of tort), Negligence is actionable by way of a civil lawsuit. Civil negligence must not be confused with Gross Negligence, which is a concept of criminal law.

Where A owes B a duty of care, and A breaches that duty in a way that causes B's death, and which falls so far below the standard of care expected from A that it should be adjudged as

---

53 [2006] EWCA Crim 17
54 [1967] 2 QB 981
55 [1966] 1 QB 59
56 Ibid, at p.70

criminal, A will be guilty of Manslaughter by Gross Negligence.

In *Broughton*[57] Lord Burnett CJ listed the now six (6) elements required for a conviction of Gross Negligence Manslaughter;

i. The Defendant must owe a duty of care to the victim
ii. The defendant must negligently breach their duty of care
iii. At the point of that breach (ii) there must have been a risk of death that was more than remote, and, immediately apparent.
iv. It was reasonably foreseeable that at the point of breach (ii) the breach gave rise to the criteria at (iii).
v. The breach at (ii) made a significant contribution to the death of the victim.
vi. The Breach at (ii) was so bad to be considered criminal.

The issues (i) – (v) are generally quite straightforward, debate generally arises when assessing whether the relevant negligence, was in fact, gross negligence (vi).

In *Bateman*[58] Lord Hewart CJ, opined that *"the facts must be such that, in the opinion of the jury, the negligence of the accused went beyond a mere matter of compensation between subjects and showed such disregard for the life and safety of others as to amount to a crime ... deserving punishment."*

It is clear from his lordship's *dicta* in *Bateman,* as well as Lord Mackay's judgment in the leading case of *Adomako*[59] that the Jury must decide whether the negligence committed by a defendant (regardless of the actual death, but with regard to the risk of death involved) is enough to be considered as a crime. Only then can the death be a matter for the criminal law.

Lord Mackay outlines in *Adomako* that *"The essence of the matter ... is whether, having regard to the risk of death involved,*

---

57 [2021] 1 Cr App R 3
58 (1925) 19 Cr App R 8
59 [1995] 1 AC 171

the conduct of the defendant was so bad in all the circumstances as to amount ... to a criminal act or omission."[60]

Helpfully, in *Misra*[61] Judge LJ, as he then was, simplified the six-ingredient list, reducing it to three (3) parts, of the same substance. He said;

"... the offence requires first, death resulting from a negligent breach of the duty of care owed by the defendant to the deceased, second, that in negligent breach of that duty, the victim was exposed by the defendant to the risk of death, and third, that the circumstances were so reprehensible as to amount to gross negligence."[62]

Final Chapter Notes

It is noteworthy that Parliament has seen fit to separate deaths which occur by way of dangerous, careless, or inconsiderate driving. As well as driving whilst not entitled to do so. Seemingly with the intention of reserving the 'manslaughter' label for the most serious offences. Some of these distinct offences are listed below;

CAUSING DEATH BY DANGEROUS DRIVING
s.1 Road Traffic Act 1988

"A person who causes the death of another person by driving a mechanically propelled vehicle dangerously on a road or other public place is guilty of an offence."

CAUSING DEATH BY CARELESS OR INCONSIDERATE DRIVING
s.2B Road Traffic Act 1988

"A person who causes the death of another person by driving a mechanically propelled vehicle on a road or other public place without

---

60 Ibid, at p.187
61 [2005] 1 Cr App R 21
62 Ibid, at [48]

due care and attention, or without reasonable consideration for other persons using the road or place, is guilty of an offence."

Causing Death by Driving: Disqualified Drivers
s.3ZC Road Traffic Act 1988

"A person is guilty of an offence under this section if he or she –
  (a) causes the death of another person by driving a motor vehicle on a road, and
  (b) at that time, is committing an offence under section 103(1)(b) of this Act (driving while disqualified)."

Causing Death by Driving: Unlicenced or Uninsured Drivers
s.3ZB Road Traffic Act 1988

"A person is guilty of an offence under this section if he causes the death of another person by driving a motor vehicle on a road and, at the time when he is driving, the circumstances are such that he is committing an offence under –

(a) section 87(1) of this Act (driving otherwise than in accordance with a licence),

(b) . . . or

(c) section 143 of this Act (using motor vehicle while uninsured . . .)."

Causing death by careless driving when under the influence of drink or drugs
s.3A Road Traffic Act 1988

"(1) If a person causes the death of another person by driving a mechanically propelled vehicle on a road or other public place without due care and attention, or without reasonable consideration for other persons using the road or place, and –

(a) he is, at the time when he is driving, unfit to drive through drink or drugs, or

(b) he has consumed so much alcohol that the proportion of it in his breath, blood or urine at that time exceeds the prescribed limit, or

(ba) he has in his body a specified controlled drug and the proportion of it in his blood or urine at that time exceeds the specified limit for that drug, or

(c) he is, within 18 hours after that time, required to provide a specimen in pursuance of section 7 of this Act, but without reasonable excuse fails to provide it, or

(d) he is required by a constable to give his permission for a laboratory test of a specimen of blood taken from him under section 7A of this Act, but without reasonable excuse fails to do so,
he is guilty of an offence.

It is further noteworthy to mention the doctrine of Joint Enterprise, which relates to when people other than the 'main offender' stand to be convicted of the 'main offence' despite not having carried out the *actus reus*. Joint enterprise generally comes into the picture where people at the scene of the crime assist or encourage the main offender. Where such an occurrence happens, the secondary offender will be convicted of the same offence as the main offender.

CHAPTER 4

Non-Fatal Offences Against the Person

Assault

Battery

Assault Occasioning Actual Bodily Harm *(s.47)*

Wounding or Inflicting Grievous Bodily Harm *(s.20)*

Wounding or Inflicting Grievous Bodily Harm
      with Intent *(s.18)*

A note on charging practices: *Severity of Injuries*

'Assault' in everyday language means any number of things, from a punch or a hit, to the infliction of a life-changing injury. But in law, the offence of Assault is much narrower. This chapter will consider some of the different types of non-fatal offences against the person.

Assault

'Assault' in law, requires no physical contact between the assailant and the victim whatsoever.

In *Ireland & Burstow*[63] Lord Steyn outlined that an assault, in law, is an action which causes the Victim to apprehend immediate and unlawful personal violence. Ireland followed on from a string of other significant cases which allowed the offence of Assault to develop in common law. Though, as confirmed in *Haystead*[64], seemingly a common law offence, Assault is, in practice charged as contrary to s.39 Criminal Justice Act 1988.

Apprehension

Apprehension of violence does not mean fear of it, it can more properly be equated to an expectation of violence. In *Logdon*[65] the Defendant threatened the victim with a toy gun. The Court of Appeal outlined that the key question as to the element of apprehension in respect of a charge of Assault was; whether or not the Victim expected to be then and there subjected to personal violence. In *Logdon*, the Victim expected the gun to be real, and therefore did apprehend some immediate and unlawful violence to befall his person. Hence, the apprehension element of the Assault was satisfied.

---

63 [1998] AC 147
64 *Haystead v Chief Constable of Derbyshire* [2000] 3 All ER 890
65 *Logdon v DPP* [1976] Crim LR 121

Immediacy

The authorities make reference to the violence (for which any contact will suffice – see discussion of 'force' below) expected being immediate. In *Constanza*[66], the court held that the word 'immediate' should be treated as if it meant *"at some time not excluding the immediate future"*. It is accepted that perhaps the most useful illustration of the concept of immediacy can be found in the case of *Smith*[67], wherein the Defendant took up position outside the Victim's home. Aware of his presence the Victim became scared of what may happen (i.e., violence) if the Defendant was able to enter. The Court of Appeal were, ultimately, faced with the question of whether the Victim could have apprehended *immediate* personal violence, given the Defendant was outside of her home. Kerr LJ, said that she could have, he explained that the expectation could be innominate, so long as it is there, and expected to occur in line with the principle in Constanza.

The relevant *mens rea* for an Assault is either, Intention or Recklessness. Making Assault a basic intent crime.

Battery

Often referred to as Assault by Beating, this again is a common law offence, and is again charged as contrary to s.39 Criminal Justice Act 1988. The relevant *mens rea* is again either, Intention or Recklessness. Making Battery a basic intent crime.

Battery is what is more typically thought of as an 'assault' in common language. It is the infliction of unlawful force upon another. It does not require any injury to be inflicted, mere unlawful contact will suffice.

---

66 [1997] 2 Cr App R 492
67 *Smith v Chief Constable of Woking Police Station* (1983) 76 Cr App R 234

Battery is most helpfully defined in *Williams*[68] by Lord Lane CJ where he outlined that Battery is to be considered; *"an act by which the Defendant, intentionally or recklessly, applies unlawful force to the [victim]."*

Force

It is useful at this stage to consider what is meant by the word 'force'. Its general language conjures some relatively meaningful acts, a punch or a slap perhaps. But in law 'force' means any touching whatsoever, including through clothing, or with an implement. The courts have confirmed, by way of an example, that the touching the hem of a skirt, even where it could not be felt by the wearer of the skirt, amounted to 'force' for the purposes of a battery.[69]

There is however a caveat to this rule, in that, force to which one is taken to expect in the course of everyday life will not amount to 'force' for the purposes of battery, the Court refers to this as acts which go beyond the *"generally acceptable standards of conduct"*[70]. His Lordship, it has been accepted, was referring to force that is generally expected to arise in the living of ordinary, everyday life, such as brushing past, or bumping into another person on a busy bus or after having lost ones footing on a moving train.

In criminal law, it is often said that context is everything – this is never truer than when considering the question of force according to the guide laid out by Goff LJ – in one circumstance the force will be acceptable, such as a shoulder bump on a busy moving train arriving at a station – but the same shoulder bump may not be considered acceptable where there is only two people in the vestibule and the train is stationary, down the line, waiting for a platform.

---

68 (Gladstone) [1987] 3 All ER 411
69 *Thomas* (1985) 81 Cr App R 331
70 *Collins v Wilcock* [1984] 3 All ER 374, Goff LJ

The force employed must be unlawful, this simply means that there must not be a lawful excuse present. This will be considered more in Chapter 13, general Defences.

Assault Occasioning Actual Bodily Harm (s.47)

Assault Occasioning Actual Bodily Harm (ABH) is a statutory offence defined by the Offences Against the Person Act 1861, s.47;

> *Whosoever shall be convicted upon an indictment of any assault occasioning actual bodily harm shall be liable*

Often referenced as simply, 'ABH', this basic intent offence is the first in the line of offences discussed in this chapter which requires some injury to be suffered by the victim.

ABH can be thought of as having three elements;

1. An intention or a state of recklessness as to the infliction of harm (*mens rea*, basic intent)
2. An Assault (either an Assault, or, and more normally, an Assault by beating)
3. That (2) occasions (causes) ABH itself.

The first and second elements have been addressed previously in this text. In relation to the causation of ABH itself, the Assault or Battery must be both the factual and legal cause of the ABH.

Meaning of ABH

ABH is considered to be 'some harm'. In law it carries the definition laid down by Lynskey J, in *Miller*[71]; *"any hurt or injury calculated to interfere with the health or comfort of the [victim]."* The

---

71 [1954] 2 QB 282

word calculated need not worry readers at this level, there is no need for any premeditation, or malicious calculation on the part of the Defendant. Calculation in this context means only 'considered' – so, some injury that is considered to impact the victim's health or comfort.

Often, it is easier to consider ABH to merely mean, 'some harm', this can be physical harm, or as confirmed in *Ireland & Burstow*[72] recognisable psychiatric harm. This text will not consider psychiatric harm in significant detail, but readers should note that mere upset, panic, or fear will not be enough to satisfy the standard of ABH.[73]

Wounding or Inflicting Grievous Bodily Harm (s.20)

A further crime of Basic Intent, Wounding or Inflicting Grievous Bodily Harm is a statutory offence, contrary to Offences Against the Person Act 1861, s.20.

There are two routes to commission of the s.20 offence. The first is Wounding, and the second is Inflicting Grievous Bodily Harm (GBH), both require that the injury be *'really serious'*[74], and unlawful (i.e., without a lawful justification). A minor wound, though technically falling within the definition of s.20, could still be charged as an offence contrary to s.47 of the 1861 Act. – more on this below.

Due regard must be given to the context of the victim's personal characteristics.[75] The editors of Blackstones' Criminal Practice 2023 furnish us with an excellent example of why; *"Injury to a finger [which might normally be considered ABH] could*

---

72 [1998] AC 147
73 *Dhaliwal* [2006] EWCA Crim 1139
74 *DPP v Smith* [1961] AC 290
75 *Bollom* [2004] 2 Cr App R 50

thus be grievous bodily harm where [the victim] is a professional musician."[76]

Wounding

A wound, is considered to be any break in either (1) the continuity of the whole skin (dermis & epidermis)[77], or, (2) the inner skin of the cheek, lip, or urethra.[78] It is often thought by students that if something bleeds that it would be a wound. That descriptor is far too simplistic – even for this text – though most wounds will bleed, not all bleeding will emanate from a wound. In *Eisenhower*[79] the victim was shot in the eye and suffered internal bleeding, as there was no break in the whole skin, nor in the relevant inner skins, there was no legal wound.

With wounding, it is a good starting point to consider the skin, if it has been broken in a significant manner (scratches will not suffice[80]), and from a practical perspective might require stiches or gluing, then there is likely a wound.

Grievous Bodily Harm (GBH)

GBH is, simply, any other bodily harm that is 'Really Serious' and is not a Wound. The really serious bodily harm does not have to be a result of a single injury, but can be the result of a culmination of minor injuries, that when taken together, amount to really serious harm. In *Birmingham*[81];

> *"There was agreed medical evidence that she was found to have a total of eleven cuts inflicted ... All the lacerations were described by the doctor who examined her as "superficial". There was one*

---

76 *Blackstones' Criminal Practice 2023, OUP* (B2.79)
77 *Moriarty v Brooks* (1834) 6 C&P 684
78 *Waltham* (1849) 3 Cox CC 442
79 *JCC (a minor) v Eisenhower* [1984] QB 331
80 *M'Loughlin* (1838) 8 C&P 635
81 [2002] EWCA Crim 2608

to her scalp, ... two to her left wrist, ...; one to the crease of her right thumb, ...; one to the back of her left hand, ... requiring three stitches to close it; two to the back of her right wrist; and four to her feet and ankles, requiring nine stitches in all. Some of the lacerations did not require stitching but were closed by Steri-strips."[82]

The decision in Birmingham is one example of where the legal and medical professions fall out of alignment, which I will add, for the benefit of the reader, happens regularly. Keene LJ went on to say;

"In medical parlance, these wounds were described as "superficial", but one required three stitches and those to the feet and ankles required nine stitches. Once one puts all that together with the number of wounds, one cannot accept that these injuries could not, as a matter of law, have amounted to serious bodily harm."

Psychiatric injury can also suffice for GBH, but, again, it must be really serious in its nature – which will ultimately, as with all questions of fact, be a matter for the jury.

Infliction

There is some debate in relation to this area, but for the purposes of this text, the word 'inflict' can be read to mean 'cause'. In *Ireland*[83] Lord Steyn established that *"there was no radical divergence between the meanings of the words 'cause' and 'inflict"*.

It stands to reason that the law relating to causation in regards to s.47, and the general criminal law, will apply equally to offences under s.20, and for that matter, s.18.

---

82 Ibid, at [7], Keene LJ
83 [1998] AC 147, at p.160

Wounding or Inflicting Grievous Bodily Harm with Intent (s.18)

The s.18 variant of GBH can be treated in exactly the same way, with regards to the *actus reus* of the offence, the only difference between s.18 and the lesser offence of s.20, detailed above, is in regards to the *mens rea*.

Wounding or Inflicting Grievous Bodily Harm with Intent, contrary to s.18 of the 1861 Act, is a crime of specific intent. This means that to be convicted of the more serious offence, a defendant must intend to inflict GBH, or intend, to wound.

The s.18 offence can also be committed where the intention is to resist arrest, or prevent a lawful arrest – this is not considered in this text, as it goes beyond the scope of a 'straightforward guide'.

A note on charging practices: *Severity of Injuries*

It is noteworthy that although any harm, that satisfies the 'some harm' test for ABH could be charged as such – in practice, ABH is only charged in circumstances where the injury is relatively serious or meaningful, but not *really serious* so as to be considered GBH. Often, minor injuries result in a charge of Assault by Beating, contrary to s.39 CJA 1988. The table overleaf may be a useful explanatory tool.

Offence	Exemplar levels of 'harm'
Assault	• D raises a fist to the V • D points a gun at the V
Battery (assault by beating)	• Push • Slap, resulting in slight reddening • Grazes • Minor bruising
s.47 ABH	• Broken nose • Hairline fractures • Loss of consciousness • Non-Really Serious Injuries resulting from kicking or the use of a weapon • Minor infections • Mild Mental Illness • Injuries requiring professional medical treatment
s.20 GBH & s.18 GBH (with intent)	• Broken major bones • Major infections • Significant gunshot wounds • Significant stab wounds • Serious mental illness • Injuries requiring prolonged professional medical treatment • Sexually transmitted infections

CHAPTER 5

Sexual Offences

Rape
Assault by Penetration
Sexual Assault
Sources of Support

Sexual offences are the most stigmatised offences in English & Welsh law. They are often considered too sensitive to teach on undergraduate university Criminal Law modules. But they are an important genre of criminal law. It is submitted that to gloss over them in the pursuit of sensitivity is an insult to survivors and undermines their position as some of the most harmful offences in our law.

It is of note that sexual offences, whilst traumatic to their victims, are, arguably, more traumatic to those who have been wrongly accused. Unlike many other offences a not-guilty verdict does not return the wrongly-accused to their pervious life. They will, in all likelihood, suffer from prolonged, even lifelong, stigma and suspicion from those aware of the allegation.

Rape

A statutory offence of specific intent. Sexual Offences Act 2003, s.1(1), provides;

> *A person (A) commits an offence if —*
> *(a) he intentionally penetrates the vagina, anus or mouth of another person (B) with his penis,*
> *(b) B does not consent to the penetration, and*
> *(c) A does not reasonably believe that B consents.*

Rape can, therefore, only be committed (as a principal) by a biological male, which includes post-operative transgender persons with a surgically constructed penis.[84]

It is clear that Rape can be distilled into 3 elements, beyond its specific intention;

- Penile penetration of a relevant orifice (vagina, anus, or, mouth)
- Without consent
- Without a reasonable belief in consent

---

[84] Sexual Offences Act 2003, s.79(3)

Penile penetration

The penile aspect of penetration is self-explanatory.

Penetration is a relatively well-understood term. In law it is described as a *"continuing act from entry to withdrawal"*.[85] It is therefore clear that penetration begins the moment the penis makes entry in to one of the relevant orifices and ends at the point of withdrawal. Multiple 'entry-exits' therefore would amount to multiple penetrations. Readers should also note that ejaculation is not relevant – the new law makes no mention of it, and the old law expressly did not require it, noting; *"it shall not be necessary to prove the completion of the intercourse by the emission of seed"*.[86]

Relevant Orifices

In respect of vaginal penetration, the word 'vagina' in law is taken to mean 'generally – female genitalia'.[87] It is now accepted that the vulva (the outer vagina) is included as are vaginas (and vulvas) which are surgically constructed – by virtue of s.79(9), and s.79(3) of the 2003 Act, respectively.

Anal and Oral penetration are similarly interpreted and are straightforward in application.

Without Consent

The discussion of consent in this chapter related to sexual offences only.

As a result of developments in understanding stigma and myths around the matter of consent, the definition of consent is now placed on a statutory footing, making the matter clearer in law. That said, juries are faced with a duty to make determinations in respect of consent. As most rapes take place

---

85 Sexual Offences Act 2003, s.79(2)
86 Sexual Offences Act 1956, s.44 (as enacted)
87 *F* [2002] EWCA Crim 2936

in the victim's home, by someone known to them, only in the presence of the complainant and the accused, it is a decision which should warrant significant caution from jurors. They will be assisted by the relevant context garnered from witnesses and, rightly or wrongly, the submissions of counsel.[88]

Consent is considered in three stages;

1. Conclusive presumptions[89]
2. Rebuttable presumptions[90]
3. General consent[91]

CONCLUSIVE PRESUMPTIONS

Where, in law, a conclusive presumption exists, if certain facts are proven then the conclusion in law, in respect of a certain question, can only reflect the presumption. In respect of consent, s.76 of the 2003 Act establishes the following presumption;

> (1) *If ... it is proved that the defendant did the relevant act and that any of the circumstances specified in subsection (2) existed, it is to be conclusively presumed –*
>   *(a) that the complainant did not consent to the relevant act, and*
>   *(b) that the defendant did not believe that the complainant consented to the relevant act.*
>
> (2) *The circumstances are that –*
>   *(a) the defendant intentionally deceived the complainant as to the nature or purpose of the relevant act;*
>   *(b) the defendant intentionally induced the complainant to consent to the relevant act by impersonating a person known personally to the complainant.**

*'relevant act', means, the actus reus of an offence to which this presumption applies (ss.1-4 of the 2003 Act).

---

88 C [2012] EWCA Crim 2034
89 Sexual Offences Act 2003, s.76
90 Sexual Offences Act 2003, s.75
91 Sexual Offences Act 2003, s.74

SEXUAL OFFENCES

In essence, s.76 provides that if a defendant either lies to the complainant in respect of either the physical act or the reason for the act, or, pretends to be, for example the complainants partner, in order to cause the complainant to consent – the court must find that the complainant did not consent to the *actus reus* and therefore the offence will have been committed.

Rebuttable Presumptions

Where a rebuttable presumption exists in law, if certain facts are proven then the conclusion in respect of the relevant question will be presumed, unless the defendant presents a valid 'rebuttal' to the presumption. In respect of consent, s.75 provides for such a rebuttable presumption;

> *(1) If in proceedings for an offence to which this section applies it is proved –*
> *(a) that the defendant did the relevant act,*
> *(b) that any of the circumstances specified in subsection (2) existed, and*
> *(c) that the defendant knew that those circumstances existed, the complainant is to be taken not to have consented to the relevant act unless sufficient evidence is adduced to raise an issue as to whether he consented, and the defendant is to be taken not to have reasonably believed that the complainant consented unless sufficient evidence is adduced to raise an issue as to whether he reasonably believed it.*
>
> *(2) The circumstances are that –*
> *(a) any person was, at the time of the relevant act or immediately before it began, using violence against the complainant or causing the complainant to fear that immediate violence would be used against him;*
> *(b) any person was, at the time of the relevant act or immediately before it began, causing the complainant to fear that violence*

> was being used, or that immediate violence would be used, against another person;
> (c) the complainant was, and the defendant was not, unlawfully detained at the time of the relevant act;
> (d) the complainant was asleep or otherwise unconscious at the time of the relevant act;
> (e) because of the complainant's physical disability, the complainant would not have been able at the time of the relevant act to communicate to the defendant whether the complainant consented;
> (f) any person had administered to or caused to be taken by the complainant, without the complainant's consent, a substance which, having regard to when it was administered or taken, was capable of causing or enabling the complainant to be stupefied or overpowered at the time of the relevant act.
>
> (3) In subsection (2)(a) and (b), the reference to the time immediately before the relevant act began is, in the case of an act which is one of a continuous series of sexual activities, a reference to the time immediately before the first sexual activity began.

Readers will see that in such a case where one of the circumstances in s.75(2) exist, the Defendant will be asked to justify either the complainant's consent, or, their own reasonable belief in the complainant's consent. If the Defendant cannot do so, the complainant will be presumed not to have consented, and the Defendant will be presumed not to have a reasonable belief in such consent. Thus, the offence, if the *actus reus* is proven, will be presumed to have been committed.

GENERAL CONSENT

If the use of ss.75-76 is not appropriate, then the fallback position is to the general rule in respect of consent, contained within s.74 of the 2003 Act, which provides;

> *a person consents if he agrees by choice, and has the freedom and capacity to make that choice.*

This is accepted to be a broad definition and allows for much more contextual analysis by a jury, than in situations falling within ss.75-76. It is submitted that this, really, should be enough and would likely result in outcomes commensurate with the provisions of ss.75-76 in the relevant circumstances – there is practically no real need for ss.75-76 – presuming juries are properly directed on relevant stereotypes and myths, and follow those directions. Which it is accepted results in a cyclical debate.

Capacity is a complex area of law in its own right, a person's lack of capacity is defined by the Mental Capacity Act 2005, s.2;

> *(1) For the purposes of this Act, a person lacks capacity in relation to a matter if at the material time he is unable to make a decision for himself in relation to the matter because of an impairment of, or a disturbance in the functioning of, the mind or brain.*
> *(2) It does not matter whether the impairment or disturbance is permanent or temporary.*

It is clear that capacity, is a factor determined by an ability to make a decision, s.3(1) of the 2005 Act further provides that;

> *For the purposes of section 2, a person is unable to make a decision for himself if he is unable –*
> *(a) to understand the information relevant to the decision,*
> *(b) to retain that information,*
> *(c) to use or weigh that information as part of the process of making the decision, or*
> *(d) to communicate his decision (whether by talking, using sign language or any other means).*

In circumstances where a complainant does not have capacity to consent, in line with the provisions of the 2005 Act, they cannot consent. Capacity is decision specific; a person may have capacity to choose what they want to wear, but not to sexual activity.

Freedom is a much simpler concept, it relates to an active decision, as opposed to submission to a course of action. In *Olugboja*[92] Dunn LJ asserted that; *"every consent involves a submission, but it by no means follows that a mere submission involves consent."* Clearly, the 'freedom' element of s.74 of the 2003 Act relates to situations where a complainant cannot exercise a free choice, perhaps because of external pressure, desperation, or even internal responses to stress.

and without a reasonable belief in consent

The phrase 'reasonable' imports objective standards into what would, *prima facie*, be a subjective element of the offence. The issue for the jury would be to determine if the Defendant actually believed that the complainant was consenting to the *actus reus* – if he did, then the jury must consider the objective element, i.e., whether a reasonable person would have believed the same, in the circumstances.

The case of *Braham*[93] provides an excellent illustration of the reasonable belief test in action. The Defendant suffered from delusions that he had healing powers, that were exercised by way of sexual activity with the person to be healed – in an effort to heal his partner he had sexual intercourse with her, without her consent. Hughes LJ, in his judgment, provided the following contextualised description of the test; *"A delusional belief in consent, if entertained, would be by definition irrational and thus unreasonable, not reasonable."*[94]

---

92   [1982] QB 320
93   [2013] EWCA Crim 3
94   Ibid, at [35], Hughes LJ

Assault by Penetration

Readers will appreciate from the above, that Rape requires penile penetration, yet a person can be, arguably equally, violated by way of digital penetration, or penetration with another object. It is to resolve this matter that the offence of Assault by Penetration was created – it carries the same maximum sentence as Rape and serves to fill the part of the lacuna left by s.1 of the 2003 Act.

A further crime of Specific Intent, s.2(1) of the 2003 Act provides that a person (A) will be guilty of an offence where;

> *(a) he intentionally penetrates the vagina or anus of another person (B) with a part of his body or anything else,*
> *(b) the penetration is sexual,*
> *(c) B does not consent to the penetration, and*
> *(d) A does not reasonably believe that B consents.*

s.2(1) is a relatively straightforward provision as it stands, but there are elements that require further development in order to properly understand their significance. The elements of the offence at s.2(1)(a), and ss.2(1)(c-d) take their meaning from the same authorities outlined as part of this text's discussion on the offence of Rape.

s.2(1)(b) however, requires further consideration, as to when something will be considered 'sexual' in law.

The starting point for the definition, is by way of an intrinsic aid to statutory interpretation, s.78 of the 2003 Act, outlines when an activity will be 'sexual', it states;

> ...*penetration, touching or any other activity is sexual if a reasonable person would consider that* –
> (a) *whatever its circumstances or any person's purpose in relation to it, it is because of its nature sexual, or*
> (b) *because of its nature it may be sexual and because of its circumstances or the purpose of any person in relation to it (or both) it is sexual.*

The use of the word "*or*" within s.78(a) demonstrates that there are two ways that conduct can be considered as sexual by virtue of the s.78 provision.

Firstly, where something is overtly and clearly sexual, regardless of motive or intent, s.78(a) will apply, and the conduct will be deemed to be sexual in law.

The more nuanced position is from within s.78(b), wherein the activity *'may' prima facie*, be sexual but, it may also not be – so consideration is then given to the defendant's purpose in committing the act, and the circumstances surrounding it.

The court in *H* [2005] 1 WLR 2005 outlined that the provision under s.78(b) contained two distinct questions, first the jury must consider if the relevant conduct (in the case of an offence under s.2; vaginal or anal penetration), *may* have been sexual. Secondly, if it *may* have been, *was it in fact* sexual. The distinction in *H* may seem trivial to readers of this guide, but it is an important one, it safeguards defendants against volatile presumptions in cases where at first glance one might conclude the conduct was sexual, but when considered in the context of the alleged offending, may be wholly innocent. It also protects victims, from conduct which may seem innocuous, but is actually sexual in its nature.

The editors of Blackstones' Criminal Practice 2023 expertly provide the typical example of when the latter scenario may arise, they say[95];

---

95 B3.60

"Section 78(b) will have the effect of making an intimate medical examination involving digital examination of the vagina or anus 'sexual' where the examination is not a bona fide examination and the doctor's purpose is sexual gratification. Arguably, even where a doctor conducts a properly required intimate medical examination, if it was conducted in an inappropriate manner, it may be concluded that the activity was 'sexual' if it can be established that the doctor had an ulterior purpose of sexual gratification. See the facts of Bolduc and Bird (1967) 63 DLR (2d) 82, where a doctor carried out a necessary examination but allowed a friend to be present for his sexual gratification."

Sexual Assault

This offence is often trivialised by society. There are countless examples of where matters that fall within the ambit of this offence are brushed to the side by both the relevant authorities and by victims themselves, often as a result of societal pressures. But readers should make no mistake, Sexual Assault is a serious offence, with serious consequences for both victims and offenders, and the wrongly accused, alike.

s.3(1) of the 2003 Act provides, a person (A) will be guilty of an offence if;

(a) he intentionally touches another person (B),
(b) the touching is sexual,
(c) B does not consent to the touching, and
(d) A does not reasonably believe that B consents.

ss.3(1)(b-c) take their meaning, again, from the above. The '*touching*' element under s.3(1)(a) requires further consideration.

"*Touching*" for the purposes of the 2003 Act is given an exceptionally wide scope by the relevant case law. It does not need to be felt; it does not need to be to the skin; touching through clothing will suffice, even if there is no pressure applied to the body itself, indirect touching will also suffice.

Even given the wide scope, however, there must still be some conduct amounting to *"touching"*, without it the offence is not completed.

s.79(8) provides an additional intrinsic aid. It states that, touching includes;

> *(a) with any part of the body,*
> *(b) with anything else,*
> *(c) through anything,*
> *and in particular includes touching amounting to penetration.*

Turning to caselaw, in *Bounekhla*[96] the defendant, without the complainant's knowledge, took out his penis and caused himself to ejaculate onto the complainant's clothing whilst, in effect 'grinding' upon her on the dancefloor. Although in *Bounekhla* the defendant pressed up against the victim and so there was direct *"touching"*, the ejaculation still constitutes *"touching"* within the meaning of the Act – applying s.79(8), the ejaculatory fluid will either amount to *"(a) any part of the body"* i.e., bodily fluid, or in the alternative, *"(b) ... anything else"*. Hence, the contact between the fluid *"through"*[97] the victim's clothing – will amount to *"touching"*.

Sources of Support

It is accepted, that perhaps more than other areas, the study of Sexual Offending can evoke strong feelings. To that end, the details overleaf may be of some use to my readers.

---

96 [2006] EWCA Crim 1217
97 Sexual Offences Act 2003, s.79(8)(c)

SEXUAL OFFENCES

Rape Crisis (England & Wales) – 0808 500 2222, rapecrisis.org.uk/get-help.

Male Survivors Partnership – 0808 800 5005

Victim Support – 0808 168 9111

If you are in danger, or require emergency help, call 999, or your local emergency number.

CHAPTER 6

Theft, Fraud & Related Offences

Theft

Robbery

Burglary

Fraud

Making off without Payment
Taking Conveyance without Authority 'TWOC'

This chapter will deal with offences of dishonesty. These offences often seem insignificant to the layperson, most images when one thinks of thieves and robbers, emanate from TV, or even childhood stories, they are romanticised. In fact, however, the commission of offences within this chapter can have an enduring impact on the lives of victims, but also on the offenders – someone with a conviction for an offence of dishonesty, however minor, is significantly disadvantaged, even after they have served their sentence. The stigma of being a thief is still a perpetually strong force.

We start with Theft.

Theft

Theft is a statutory offence of specific intention. It requires five elements to be satisfied. Those elements are laid down in the Theft Act 1968, s.1(1), which outlines;

> A person is guilty of theft if he dishonestly appropriates property belonging to another with the intention of permanently depriving the other of it; and "thief" and "steal" shall be construed accordingly.

The five elements can, therefore, be effectively broken down as follows;

- Dishonesty
- Appropriation
- Property
- Belonging to another
- With intention to permanently deprive

Dishonesty

Unhelpfully, when Parliament passed the 1968 Act only a negative definition of dishonesty was included. So, in essence, the statute only tells us when someone is *"not to be regarded as dishonest"*[98]. The relevant section[99] outlines three circumstances where a defendant will not be dishonest, they are;

> *(a) if he appropriates the property in the belief that he has in law the right to deprive the other of it, on behalf of himself or a third person; or*
> *(b) if he appropriates the property in the belief that he would have the other's consent if the other knew of the appropriation and the circumstances of it; or*
> *(c) (except where the property came to him as trustee or personal representative) if he appropriates the property in the belief that the person to whom the property belongs cannot be discovered by taking reasonable steps.*

These 'honesty provisions' are relatively self-explanatory; they can be expressed in a simplified manner as follows;

(a) The defendant believes he, or a third party on whose behalf he acts, has a right to appropriate the property.
(b) The defendant believes that the appropriation would be consented to, if the person to be deprived knew of the circumstances of the appropriation.
(c) Effectively, *'finders' keepers, losers' weepers.'* But with the condition that the *'finder'* must believe that the *'loser'* cannot be discovered by taking reasonable steps.

If one of these provisions applies then the defendant will, by law, be considered as not dishonest, and therefore cannot be convicted of Theft, as he falls at the first element of dishonesty.

It does not follow however that the Defendant will then be considered dishonest if none of the 'honesty provisions' apply. As, if none of the 'honesty provisions' apply, then the

---

[98] Theft Act 1968, s.2(1)
[99] Theft Act 1968, s.2(1)(a-c)

court must move to determine whether the defendant will be considered dishonest.

The mechanism for determining dishonesty has changed over time, but is now, for the time-being at least, in a stable state. In *Ivey*[100] the UK Supreme Court considered former caselaw on the matter of when someone will be considered dishonest. The court found significant flaws with the former cases, and overruled caselaw which had stood since the 1980s. The new *Ivey* test for dishonesty is a two-part test, and was confirmed to apply in criminal cases[101];

In applying *Ivey*, the court must consider;

1. What did the Defendant think the relevant facts were?
2. Given the Defendant's believe as to the facts, was he dishonest according to the reasonable standards of ordinary people?

If the answer to the second question is no, then the Defendant will not be dishonest in law, and cannot be convicted. If the answer is yes, however, the court will be satisfied that the defendant was dishonest and will then move to consider the remaining elements of the offence of Theft.

Appropriation

This is the 'taking' element of the offence. But in actuality, in order to appropriate an item, the defendant need not take it at all. What they must do however, is assume at least one of the rights that the owner of the property would have.[102] There is some debate as to whether a defendant need assume more than one right (said debate surrounds the fact that s.3 of the 1968 Act

---

100 *Ivey v Genting Casinos (UK) Ltd t/a Crockfords [2018] AC 391*
101 *Barton; Booth* [2020] EWCA Crim 575
102 Theft Act 1968, s.3

refers to *"rights"* rather than *"right"*) but the caselaw suggests that the assumption of a single right will suffice.[103]

Assumption of a right of an owner has taken many forms in the associated caselaw, by way of a few illustrations, all of the following would be an appropriation;

- Changing price tags on items in a shop.
- Picking up an item
- Moving an item from one place to another
- Destroying an item

Property

To some this may appear as straightforward, and to a certain extent it is. Nevertheless, it is important that it is discussed in a little detail.

Property, for the purposes of the 1968 Act, is defined by s.4(1), which states;

> *'Property' includes money and all other property, real or personal, including things in action and other intangible property.*

There are relevant provisions in relation the theft of Land, but said provisions fall outside the scope of this text.

In essence, and from a practical perspective, one should assume that everything is property, and is capable of being stolen, until proven otherwise, such proof will arise out of specific exceptions. By way of illustration, s.4(4) of the 1968 Act outlines that although wild creatures will be considered property, in law, they cannot be stolen unless they have been *"reduced into possession"*. Thus, in essence, they do not fall to be treated as property, in law, until they have been taken into possession as property.

A further illustration is in respect of human remains. The bodies of the deceased, generally, are not considered property

---

[103] *Gomez* [1993] AC 442

in law, unless they have been subjected to special skills in order to further purposes of exhibition or education.[104]

It may be noteworthy to readers of this text that electricity can also not be stolen.[105] However, the criminal law, as it often does, provides an alternative route to conviction, in this case, by virtue of the offence of Abstraction.[106]

Belonging to Another

Many readers will be familiar with the expression that asserts that possession is nine-tenths of the law. This is a significant oversimplification of the law but does hold some truth.

In respect of the 1968 Act, property will 'belong to another' if the 'other' has possession or control of it, or indeed any proprietary right or interest.[107] Put simply, it is possible for something to belong to another, even if they are not the valid owner. It does not matter if the person in possession has come into such possession unlawfully.[108]

It is desirable to mention a few illustrations in respect of so-called, 'abandoned' property. Abandonment is an elusive option for the lay person to understand. In law, to be abandoned it must be clear that the abandoner, has relinquished all interests or rights in the property.

In *Ricketts*[109] donations were left outside a charity shop. The defendant collected those bags for his own gain. It was submitted by Rickett's legal team that, in essence the property had been abandoned – the court disagreed, Wyn Williams J held;

---

104 *Kelly* [1999] QB 621
105 *Low v Blease* [1975] Crim LR 513
106 Theft Act 1968, s.13
107 Theft Act 1968, s.5
108 *Smith (Michael Andrew)* [2011] EWCA Crim 66
109 *R (on the application of Ricketts) v Basildon Magistrates' Court* [2010] EWHC 2358 (Admin)

> *"However, it is clearly the case, in my judgment, that it was open to the court to infer that the items had not been abandoned. The obvious inference on the bare facts before the magistrates was that person's unknown had intended the goods to be a gift to the British Heart Foundation. Those persons had an intention to give; they had also attempted to effect delivery. Delivery would be complete however only when the British Heart Foundation took possession of the items. Until that time, although the unknown would-be donor had divested himself of possession of the items, he had not given up his ownership of the items."*

Finally in respect of 'belonging to another', it would be a significant disservice not to outline that where a person comes into possession of property by error, that person is under an obligation to make restoration. In order to combat situations like this, s.5(4) was enacted as part of the 1968 Act, it provides;

> *Where a person gets property by another's mistake, and is under an obligation to make restoration (in whole or in part) of the property or its proceeds or of the value thereof, then to the extent of that obligation the property or proceeds shall be regarded (as against him) as belonging to the person entitled to restoration, and an intention not to make restoration shall be regarded accordingly as an intention to deprive that person of the property or proceeds.*

In *A-G's Ref (No.1 of 1983)*[110] the Defendant was overpaid wages in respect of her employment, in the amount of £74.74, the Court held she had 'got' property by her employer's mistake – and as such the property she had 'got' belonged to her employer, as they are legally-entitled to the restoration. The same does not apply to bookmakers – as wagers are not recoverable in law.[111]

---

110 [1985] QB 182
111 Gaming Act 1845, XVIII

With intention to permanently deprive

This is a relatively simple element. If, at the time of the dishonest appropriation of the property which belongs to another, a defendant intended to permanently deprive the other person of the property, then the final element will be satisfied, and such a defendant will stand capable of conviction.

In *Mitchell*[112] the defendant partook in a violent carjacking but abandoned the car a few miles down the road from the site of the offence. Charged with, and convicted of, Robbery (see below), the defendant appealed on the basis that he did not intend to permanently deprive the victim of the car. The Criminal Division of the Court of Appeal allowed his appeal, as it was clear that without an intention to permanently deprive, there could be no conviction for Robbery (for which the commission of a Theft is required).

Robbery

To 'rob', or to be 'robbed', in everyday vernacular is often thought of as simple theft. But in law, Robbery is a specific offence. Put simply, it is the commission of a Theft (as above), combined with the use (or threat) of violence.

Robbery is a statutory offence, of specific intent – but there must also be a level of *mens rea* of at least recklessness, as to the use or threat of force. The Theft Act 1968, s.8(1) establishes that;

> *A person is guilty of robbery if he steals, and immediately before or at the time of doing so, and in order to do so, he uses force on any person or puts or seeks to put any person in fear of being then and there subjected to force.*

Robbery can be broken down, therefore, into essentially, four elements;

---

112 [2008] EWCA Crim 850

- Theft
- Force on any person / causes or seeks to cause fear of force
- Immediately before, or at the time of
- In order to steal

Theft

The requirement for a Theft to be committed as a precursor to Robbery is a simple issue. If a defendant satisfies the requirements of the offence of Theft, then the first element of Robbery will be satisfied. Without a Theft, there can be no robbery. By way of an illustration, in Robinson[113] the court considered that where a defendant uses force to appropriate property which he believes he is entitled to, there will be no Theft, and, hence, no Robbery – as the Defendant would not be acting dishonestly, by virtue of the s.2 'honesty provisions'.

Force

Dawson[114] established that the word *"force"* in s.8 is a word that is ordinarily understood and requires no special interpretation, as juries will understand it. Force may be indirect, such as the grabbing of a shopping bag[115], but is seems that there must be a sufficient level of indirect force. In *P*[116] the Court held that snatching a cigarette out of a hand, was to be equated with pickpocketing, and as such is not to be considered Robbery for the purposes of s.8 of the 1968 Act. It would serve readers to bear in mind that Robbery is a very serious offence, so the level of force will ordinarily equate to that severity.

---

113 [1977] Crim LR 173
114 (1976) 64 Cr App R 170
115 *Clouden* [1987] Crim LR 56
116 *P v DPP* [2013] 1 WLR 2337

Immediately before, or at the time of

It is crucial when considering potential Robbery cases to ensure that it is identified when the Theft element was completed. This is because the statutory timeline laid down in s.8 requires the force element to be satisfied either immediately before the Theft, or at the time of the Theft itself. Force used or apprehension of force caused, after the commission of the Theft will give rise to a separate charge.

In order to steal

The force element must be satisfied, with purpose. The relevant purpose here is to commit Theft. If the force is used for some other reason, then there will be no Robbery. In *Donaghy*[117] the defendant demanded that the victim drive him to a destination, the demand was accompanied by a threat of force. Once the defendant arrived, he stole money from the driver. The defendant was found not guilty of Robbery, as his threat was made in order to travel, not in order to steal the money.

Confusion appears where there is a question of whether the force element was satisfied in order to steal, or to escape. This is often a difficult question for juries to answer and is highly fact sensitive.

Burglary

Burglary is generally thought of by lay persons as where a person breaks into a building and steals from within. Whilst this, in some cases, is correct there is much more to the offence of Burglary, which often causes confusion for students and juries alike. There is much need for reform in this area, to simplify the law and afford a more accurate, and fair, label to offenders.

There are two types of Burglary, both are offences of specific

---

117 *Donaghy and Marshall* [1981] Crim LR 644

intent, and both are based in statute. They are distinguished, not by name, but by section numbers.

s.9(1)(a) Burglary – the 'intention' variant
s.9(1)(b) Burglary – the 'doing' variant

The 'base of Burglary'

There are elements of Burglary which are common to both variants of the offence, they are;

- Entry
- A building, or part of a building,
- As a trespasser

Entry

Burglary requires a defendant to enter a building or part of a building. The 'Entry' element may seem straightforward at first glance, but in fact there are two points to consider.

Firstly, the entry must be 'effective'[118], this means that their body must have actually crossed into the building or part of a building. Further, it must be 'deliberate'[119] meaning that accidental entry will not be an 'entry' within the meaning of s.9 of the 1968 Act.

Building or part of a building

The 1968 Act does not define the word 'building'. Something which many may consider straightforward, the law in this area has developed with some convolution.

The Act does provide some assistance, s.9(4) provides that inhabited vehicles, or vessels, shall be considered buildings, but it does not go much further than that.

---

118 *Brown (Vincent)* [1985] Crim LR 212
119 *Collins* [1973] QB 100

Caselaw is the source of most assistance in this area; in *Stevens*[120], Byles J, held that; a building is *"a structure of considerable size and intended to be permanent or at least to endure for a considerable period"*.

The editors of Blackstone's Criminal Practice 2023 provide an indicative summary, they say;

"Such structures need not be inhabited, nor need they have doors, windows or foundations. A garden shed, a multi-storey car park and a [portacabin] office might each be regarded as a building, although the status of a tent is doubtful."[121]

It is noteworthy that s.9 can be made out by entry into a part of a building. This is important, as it covers where a person may enter a building, such as a university block, not as a trespasser, but then a part of the building, such as a lecturer's office, as a trespasser. His 'entry' to the building, would not have been as a trespasser, but his entry into the part of a building, would be.

Such 'part of a building' should be clearly identifiable as separate to the rest of the building, or other 'parts' of the building. In *Walkington*[122] the defendant had gone behind a shop counter – the court held that as there was a physical partition, and implied prohibition on customer's entry, it could be considered to be 'part of a building' within the meaning of the 1968 Act.

As a trespasser

The defendant must have known that he was a trespasser or have been reckless as to his status as a trespasser, at the time he entered the building, he must also, in fact, have been a trespasser.

A defendant will be a trespasser where he enters without permission, or in excess of any permission granted to him. In

---

120   *Stevens v Gourley (1859) CBNS 99*
121   B4.84
122   [1979] 2 All ER 716

Jones[123] the defendant had permission to enter a house, but then went onto steal from that house, the Court held that the defendant had acted in excess of the permission given, i.e., they had permission to enter, but not to remove property.

A person, having entered lawfully a building or part of a building, who then fulfils the rest of the elements of the offence once inside, cannot be said to have committed burglary as he did not 'enter as a trespasser'.

The variants

As already mentioned, there are two variants of the s.9 offence. These will be discussed below. They involve the addition of distinct elements to the 'base of burglary' (entering a building or part of a building as a trespasser).

The two variants are represented mathematically below;

Base of Burglary + intention to either commit therein; theft, GBH, or Criminal Damage = s.9(1)(a)

Base of Burglary + commission therein of; theft or GBH= s.9(1)(b)

s.9(1)(A) – THE INTENTION VARIANT

To fulfil the s.(9)(1)(a) offence, in addition to the elements of the Base of Burglary a defendant must, at the time of entry, intend, once they have entered, to commit one of the specified offences, contained within s.9(2);

> *The offences referred to in subsection (1)(a) above are offences of stealing anything in the building or part of a building in question, of inflicting on any person therein any grievous bodily harm... therein, and of doing unlawful damage to the building or anything therein.*[124]

---

123 *(John)* [1976] 3 All ER 54
124 Theft Act 1968, s.9(2)

Reference should be made at this stage to the three offences contained within s.9(2), they take their ordinary legal meaning, therefore readers should direct their eyes to the sections of this text dealing with; Inflicting GBH, Theft, and Criminal Damage.

If a defendant committed the base of burglary and satisfied the further 'add-on' discussed here, then they will be guilty of s.9(1)(a) Burglary.

S.9(1)(B) – THE DOING VARIANT

Operating in a similar way to s.9(1)(a), s.9(1)(b), adds a further element on to the base of burglary. In this case, the commission of a relevant offence, s.9(1)(b) reads;

> *having entered any building or part of a building as a trespasser he steals or attempts to steal anything in the building or that part of it or inflicts or attempts to inflict on any person therein any grievous bodily harm.*

Clearly therefore, if a defendant commits the base of burglary, and then, following entry, commits Theft[125], or attempts to inflict, or inflicts GBH[126], then they will be guilty of a s.9(1)(b) Burglary. Again, readers should direct their attention to the GBH and Theft sections of this text for further explanation of the elements of those offences.

Fraud

Fraud is a conduct crime, the victim does not have to suffer loss, it is the fraudulent act itself which is criminalised. This safeguards against fraudulent behaviour which is detected and then the loss averted, if a loss was required, then there would be a significant portion of offending behaviour which could go unpunished.

---

125 Theft Act 1968, s.1(1)
126 Offences Against the Person Act 1861, ss.18 & 20.

Fraud is a singular offence with three modes of satisfaction. The offence of Fraud is based in statute[127] and is an offence of specific intention. In essence this means that there are three ways to commit Fraud, identified in s.1(2) of the 2006 Act, they are;

- Fraud by false representation
- Fraud by failing to disclose information
- Fraud by abuse of position

This text will only cover Fraud by false representation, in the interests of brevity and simplicity – readers are directed to the suggested further reading outlined at the end of this text for information in respect of the further two modes of commission.

Fraud by false representation

This is the type of fraud most often evoked when reference to the s.1 offence is made. The relevant elements of Fraud by false representation are outlined in s.2(1) of the 2006 Act, which reads;

> *(a) dishonestly makes a false representation, and*
> *(b) intends, by making the representation –*
>   *(i) to make a gain for himself or another, or*
>   *(ii) to cause loss to another or to expose another to a risk of loss.*

The false representation variant of the s.1 offence can, therefore, be broken down as follows.

A defendant must;

- dishonestly
- make a false representation
- in order to either,
  - make a gain,
  - cause loss to another, or,
  - expose another to a risk of loss.

---

127 Fraud Act 2006, s.1

Dishonesty

Dishonesty for the purposes of Fraud is taken from the law of Theft, readers should revisit the dishonesty section above in this regard.

Make a false representation

A representation is defined in s.2(3) of the 2006 act, which states;

> *'Representation' means any representation as to fact or law, including a representation as to the state of mind of —*
> *(a) the person making the representation, or*
> *(b) any other person.*

Thus, any statement which may be express or implied[128] will amount to a representation.

Per s.2(2) of the 2006 Act, a representation will be false if;

> *(a) it is untrue or misleading, and*
> *(b) the person making it knows that it is, or might be, untrue or misleading.*

Such a representation will be 'made' as soon as it is 'transmitted'; by uttering, writing, conduct, or otherwise. There is no need for the representation to actually be communicated to anyone.[129]

The representation may be made to a machine[130], an example often given in this regard is when a person presents a card to a contactless card reader – by doing so they represent to the machine that they are the cardholder. If they are not, their representation will be false.

---

128   Fraud Act 2006, s.2(4)
129   *Treacy v DPP* [1971] AC 537.
130   Fraud Act 2006, s.2(5)

In order to ...

This element can be read in accordance with the ordinary meanings of the words in the statute. Specific regard should be given to s.5 of the 2006 Act, which reads, *inter alia*;

> (2) Gain" and "loss" —
>   (a) extend only to gain or loss in money or other property;
>   (b) include any such gain or loss whether temporary or permanent; and "property" means any property whether real or personal (including things in action and other intangible property).
> (3) "Gain" includes a gain by keeping what one has, as well as a gain by getting what one does not have.
> (4) "Loss" includes a loss by not getting what one might get, as well as a loss by parting with what one has.

It is important to note that there is no requirement for any actual gain or any actual loss. Thomas, in his commentary, citing the decision in *Gilbert*[131], rightly notes that; *"The victim is, in a sense, irrelevant"*[132]

Making off without Payment

This is a well-known offence; it is often referred to as 'bailing on a bill' or 'bill skipping'. In essence, it is an offence of dishonestly not paying what you must, at the time you must. There is some overlap between this offence, and other offences of dishonesty. This offence works well in some fairly specific scenarios, this text will concentrate on those.

---

131 [2012] EWCA Crim 2392
132 Thomas M, "Fraud and Related Offences," Criminal Law (3rd edn. Hall & Stott)

Making off is a statutory offence, of specific intent, contrary to s.3(1) of the Theft Act 1978[133], which states;

> ... *a person who, knowing that payment on the spot for any goods supplied or service done is required or expected from him, dishonestly makes off without having paid as required or expected and with intent to avoid payment of the amount due shall be guilty of an offence.*

Thus, the offence under s.3 of the 1978 Act can be broken down into three elements;

- Knowing payment on the spot was due
- Dishonestly makes off
- With intent to avoid payment of the amount due

Knowing payment on the spot was due

Regard should, at this stage, be given to s.3(2) of the 1978 Act, which outlines that;

> *For purposes of this section "payment on the spot" includes payment at the time of collecting goods on which work has been done or in respect of which service has been provided.*

This partial definition provides some guidance, in essence, the meaning of the 'spot' is taken to mean the place where payment is to be made. The court outlined in *Aziz*[134] that if the payment due, was in relation to a taxi ride, then the 'spot' for the purposes of s.3 would be the place where the taxi stands at the time the meter is stopped and payment sought.

---

133 Readers should note: the Theft Act 1968, and the Theft Act 1978, are two distinct pieces of legislation.
134 [1993] Crim LR 708

'Making off'

These words take their ordinary everyday meaning. In *McDavitt*[135] the court concluded that 'making off' ordinarily means leaving the premises concerned – such as where a defendant has eaten at a restaurant the restaurant would be the relevant spot. If a defendant is stopped before leaving the restaurant, then this would normally be considered as an attempted offence. That being said, the fact of making off, is ultimately a matter of fact, and juries should be directed to make a fact-specific decision in each case.

Dishonesty

Again, this takes its meaning from the law of Theft, and readers should direct their attention above.

With intent to avoid payment

In *Allen*[136] the court established that the defendant must intend not to pay, if a defendant intends to pay at a later stage, the offence will not be made out.

Taking Conveyance without Authority 'TWOC'

Often referred to as TWOC (taking without consent), and colloquially referred to as 'joyriding' – this is an offence where there is no intention to permanently deprive the person of the conveyance in question, and hence, cannot be a theft.

This offence combats 'joyriding' and 'carjacking', where the defendant does not intend to permanently deprive.

Per s.12 Theft Act 1968;

---

135 [1981] Crim LR 843
136 [1985] AC 1029

> ...*a person shall be guilty of an offence if, without having the consent of the owner or other lawful authority, he takes any conveyance for his own or another's use or, knowing that any conveyance has been taken without such authority, drives it or allows himself to be carried in or on it.*

Seemingly, the offence can be satisfied by two routes;

- Taking the conveyance without authority for his own or another's use, or,
- Driving, or allowing himself to be carried in, a conveyance, which he knows to have been taken without lawful authority.

Conveyance

The meaning of conveyance is provided by statute, s.12(7)(a) asserts;

> *"conveyance" means any conveyance constructed or adapted for the carriage of a person or persons whether by land, water or air, except that it does not include a conveyance constructed or adapted for use only under the control of a person not carried in or on it*

In layman's terms, s.12(7)(a) gives the word 'conveyance' the meaning of the word 'non-remotely controlled vehicle'. The statute also excludes pedal cycles[137], for which a separate, technical, offence, under s.12(5) of the 1968 Act, would be committed.

Taking for his own or another's use.

The conveyance in question must be 'taken'. This requires movement of the conveyance itself.[138] It is not required that the

---
137 Theft Act 1968, s.12(5)
138 *Bogacki* [1973] QB 832

defendant used the conveyance to 'take' the conveyance, they may take the conveyance by another means, such as towing, or the use of a trailer.[139]

The conveyance must be taken for the defendant's (or another's) use, as a conveyance.[140]

Driving or allowing himself to be carried

The word 'drives' takes its ordinary meaning, it is taken in the general sense; so, if the conveyance is a boat or a plane, 'drive' would mean pilot, if a motorcycle, 'drive' would mean to ride, *etc.*

Being 'carried' in or on a conveyance, requires that there be some movement of the said conveyance, whilst the defendant is in, or on, said conveyance. Just merely having gotten into a stationary conveyance, is no offence, there must be some movement.[141]

Without lawful authority

This element essentially amounts to either; the owner's consent, or another lawful authority. It must be a true consent, not a mere submission, in the context of an offence under s.12 of the 1968 Act, a violent car-jacking, would satisfy the 'without lawful authority' provision – as the wilful giving up of the vehicle, would be a submission, rather than a true consent. The defendant must also know (or be wilfully blind to the fact) that the conveyance had been taken without such authority. If a defendant merely suspects that the conveyance was taken without such authority then no offence under s.12 will be committed.[142]

---

139 *Pearce* [1973] Crim LR 321
140 *Stokes* [1983] RTR 59
141 *Diggin* (1980) 72 Cr App R 204
142 *Boldizsar v Knight* [1980] Crim LR 653

CHAPTER 7

Damage to Property

Criminal Damage
Arson
Aggravated Criminal Damage & Aggravated Arson

Historically, the law was heavily weighted towards the protection of property. Indeed, there has been much development in respect of the laws relating to criminal damage. This chapter will consider the three main offences, which in essence, flow from one another. You will see that they have many common elements.

Criminal Damage

Criminal Damage is a statutory offence of basic intent.
Per, Criminal Damage Act 1971, s.1(1);

> *A person who without lawful excuse destroys or damages any property belonging to another intending to destroy or damage any such property or being reckless as to whether any such property would be destroyed or damaged shall be guilty of an offence.*

Hence therefore, the offence of criminal damage (referred to in the statute as 'destroying or damaging property') can be separated into its component *actus reus* elements thusly;

- Without lawful excuse
- Destroys or Damages
- Property belonging to another

Without lawful excuse
It is established by s.5 of the 1971 Act that a person will be considered to have a lawful excuse when;

- They believed the person who could consent to the damage or destruction had consented, or would consent if they knew the circumstances, or,
- They were protecting their own property, or proprietary right, or those of another, which were in need of immediate

protection, and, the means of protection were reasonable in all the circumstances.

Common sense is generally the overarching factor to be considered in determining lawful excuse. If the 'excuse' falls under s.5 then, naturally, it will be lawful. But it may also be lawful if it falls outside the scope of s.5. General defences of self-defence and duress apply to Criminal Damage. Caselaw provides some helpful illustrations; it is established that a motorist, who has parked on land where wheel clamping is in lawful operation, who damages the clamp to free his car, will not have a lawful excuse.[143] Nor will the damaging of property in protest.[144]

Destroys or Damages

Destroys – destruction is a high threshold; it is much safer for prosecutors to charge 'damage'. This is because destruction includes irrevocability, if something can be repaired it has not been destroyed. The destruction must be, final, and total.[145]

Damage – is a much lower bar, it is to do with usefulness, and value. In *Hardman*[146] the court held that where a defendant painted the pavement and said paint would have washed away with the rain, but the local authority chose to pay to have it professionally removed – there would be damage. This was on the basis that there would be the lapse of time, and expenditure of funds to rectify the issue.

Auld LJ in *Morphitis*[147] explained the principle of damage succinctly, he said; *"where the owner is left, albeit temporarily,*

---

143 *Lloyd v DPP* [1992] 1 All ER 982
144 *Hutchinson v DPP* (2000) *Independent*, 20 November 2000.
145 *Barnet LBC v Eastern Electricity Board* [1973] 1 WLR 430
146 *Hardman v Chief Constable of Avon and Somerset Constabulary* [1986] Crim LR 330
147 *Morphitis v Salmon* [1990] Crim LR 48

with an incomplete article which does not fully serve the purpose that it did before ... there has clearly been damage to the article as a whole." Though this passage was in relation to the removal or tampering of articles from a working machine, it is clear that it can also be applied more generally in relation to the 'usefulness' test in respect of Criminal Damage.

Property belonging to another

Property – it is noteworthy that the definition of property in relation to criminal damage is different to that of property in respect of Theft. Property within the meaning of s.1 of the 1971 Act relates to any real, or personal property which is tangible. It includes, money, wild creatures (tamed, or usually held in captivity), but not wild organic matter.[148]

Readers should note that whilst software or digital files are clearly not property, where a digital file is corrupted or erased, it is the physical memory card, or storage device, that is considered to be 'damaged'.[149]

Belonging to another – this is relatively simple, for the purposes of this text, *per* s.10 of the 1971 Act, property will belong to any person;

> *(a) having the custody or control of it;*
> *(b) having in it any proprietary right or interest (not being an equitable interest arising only from an agreement to transfer or grant an interest); or*
> *(c) having a charge on it.*

It is clear therefore that, in most cases, the 'belonging to another' element will not be something that presents too much of an issue.

---

148 Criminal Damage Act 1971, s.10
149 *Whitley* (1991) 93 Cr App R 25

Arson

Arson is, essentially, a variant of criminal damage. Represented mathematically below;

Criminal Damage + caused by fire = Arson

Aggravated Criminal Damage & Aggravated Arson

Aggravated Criminal Damage, or Aggravated Arson, when the damage is by fire, is a more serious version of the simple offences discussed above, whereby there is an intention to endanger human life, or recklessness, as to whether human life is endangered, but there are some key differences.

Firstly, the 'lawful excuse' element discussed above does not apply in the same way. It logically follows that the lawful protection of property, or destruction of property by consent (which would make something that would otherwise be criminal, lawful), cannot, as a matter of morality, operate as a defence to endangering human life. The general defence of self-defence, however, would still apply.

Secondly, the aggravated offence does not require the property that is damaged or destroyed to belong to another.

Thirdly, and most distinctly, the defendant must have basic intent (either intention or recklessness) to either endanger life (intention), or as to whether life is endangered (recklessness). 'Life' here refers to the life of another, rather than a defendant's own life.[150]

Fourthly, in respect of the endangerment to life – the 'endangerment' intended, or the 'endangerment' in respect of which a defendant was reckless, must result from the damage itself, not merely the action of the defendant. In *Steer*[151] the

---
150 *Thakar* [2010] EWCA Crim 2136
151 [1988] AC 111

defendant shot a bullet through a window. The court held that although the defendant was reckless as to endangering life by shooting, he was not reckless as to endangering life by the causing of broken glass, and therefore could not be guilty of aggravated criminal damage. Thomas, in his book which I recommend at the end of this text, provides further discussion of this point, with excellent clarity – such discussion is beyond the scope of this straightforward guide.

CHAPTER 8

Drug Offences

Possession of a controlled drug 'simple possession'
Supply of (or offering to supply) a controlled drug
Possession of a controlled drug with intent to supply

By way of background, there have been some fundamental developments in respect of drug laws in the UK. The Misuse of Drugs Act 1971 is the principal statute with which this chapter is concerned. Though as drug manufacturing became more chemically sophisticated the need for a broader scope of coverage was answered by the Psychoactive Substances Act 2016.

This straightforward guide will focus on the offences contained within the 1971 Act, but those readers wishing to gain a fuller understanding of modern drug laws, should not underestimate the importance of the 2016 Act.

Possession of a controlled drug 'simple possession'

Simple possession is an extremely common offence, it is a conduct crime, the mere possession is enough. By way of *mens rea*, the defendant must have the knowledge of possession of something (which is in fact a controlled drug). This is neither a crime of basic or specific intention, the relevant *mens rea* is knowledge.

By virtue of s.5(1) and s.5(2) of the 1971 Act;

> *(1) ..., it shall not be lawful for a person to have a controlled drug in his possession.*
> *(2) ..., it is an offence for a person to have a controlled drug in his possession in contravention of subsection (1) above.*

Controlled Drug

The phrase, 'controlled drug' is restrictive in nature, this is the key difference between the manner in which the 1971 and 2016 Acts operate. The 2016 Act outlaws substances based on the effect which they have on the body, whereas, the 1971 Act outlaws the specific substances themselves.

Thusly, to be a controlled drug, the substance or product in question must be specified in Parts I-III of Schedule 2 of the 1971 Act. The phrases 'Class A', 'Class B', and 'Class C' are often used. For clarity, class A drugs are specified in Part I, Class B in Part II, and Class C in Part III.

Possession

To be convicted a defendant must be in 'possession' of the controlled drug. Lord Hope outlined that there are two elements to possession. First, the defendant must have some custody or control of the drug. Second, the defendant must be aware that they are in possession of the controlled drug (they do not need to know it is, specifically, a controlled drug of a specific type).[152]

Dealing with the first point of custody or control – Lord Diplock outlined in *Brooks*[153] that something is in 'possession' where *"one has in one's possession whatever is, to one's knowledge, physically in one's custody or under one's physical control"*.[154]

The 1971 Act goes somewhat further than Lord Diplock's, physical definition. The 1971 Act provides that; *"the things which a person has in his possession shall be taken to include any thing subject to his control which is in the custody of another"*.[155] Clearly therefore where a dealer has another 'hold their stash', but the 'stash' remains under the dealers control, the said dealer can properly be said to have the 'stash' in their possession.

It is noteworthy, that where a defendant is in possession of a container, the defendant will be taken to also be in possession of the contents of the container. This point is developed by Lord Clyde, in *Lambert*.

---

152 *Lambert* [2002] AC 545
153 *DPP v Brooks* [1974] AC 862
154 Ibid, at p.866H
155 Misuse of Drugs Act 1971, s.37(3)

> "Where the drug is in a container, it is sufficient for the prosecution to prove that the defendant had control of the container, that he knew of its existence and that there was something in it"[156]

Turning to the knowledge of the possession; there is a requirement that a defendant be aware of the possession itself, but they do not need to know what they are in possession of. Lord Clyde demonstrates the point eloquently, again, in *Lambert*;

> 'The second element involves that the defendant knows that the thing in question is under his control. He need not know what its nature is, but so long as he knows that the thing, whatever it is, is under his control, it is in his possession'

Specific Defences

That being said, there is an often-overlooked provision contained within statute, s.28(3)(b)(i) of the 1971 Act provides that, in respect of relevant offences (of which s.5(2) is one), a defendant shall not be convicted where;

> ...he proves that he neither believed nor suspected nor had reason to suspect that the substance or product in question was a controlled drug

Simply put therefore, if a defendant proves that they didn't know or suspect (and did not have any reason to suspect) that the item they knew to be in their possession, was a controlled drug – then they will not be guilty of the offence.

The provisions in s.28 do provide for further technical defences, but those defences fall outside the scope of this straightforward guide.

So, readers may consider, what happens to the parent or the teacher who takes drugs from a child in their charge? The answer is one of the examples wherein the law provides a

---

156 [2002] AC 545, at [126]

straightforward answer to the issue, and not only that, but an answer which reflects common sense.

The answer is provided by way of s.5(4) of the 1971 Act, which establishes a specific defence to simple possession; it provides;

> *(a) that, knowing or suspecting it to be a controlled drug, he took possession of it for the purpose of preventing another from committing or continuing to commit an offence in connection with that drug and that as soon as possible after taking possession of it he took all such steps as were reasonably open to him to destroy the drug or to deliver it into the custody of a person lawfully entitled to take custody of it; or*
> *(b) that, knowing or suspecting it to be a controlled drug, he took possession of it for the purpose of delivering it into the custody of a person lawfully entitled to take custody of it and that as soon as possible after taking possession of it he took all such steps as were reasonably open to him to deliver it into the custody of such a person.*

This defence covers people who, in effect, confiscate drugs to prevent offending (s.5(4)(a)), or come into possession of a controlled drug for the purpose of surrendering the drug to a person who could legally take control of it (s.5(4)(b)).

Supply of (or offering to supply) a controlled drug

Often referred to as 'dealing', the offence of supply is created by virtue of s.4(3) of the 1971 Act, which must be read in conjunction with s.4(1)(b) of the same Act.

It is established by s.4(1)(b) that the supply of, or offer to supply another with, a controlled drug will be unlawful. But it is s.4(3) which creates the offence, by stipulating that;

> it is an offence for a person—
> (a) to supply or offer to supply a controlled drug to another in contravention of subsection (1) above; or
> (b) to be concerned in the supplying of such a drug to another in contravention of that subsection; or
> (c) to be concerned in the making to another in contravention of that subsection of an offer to supply such a drug.

This text will not focus on the 'being concerned' variants of the offence, so will therefore focus on s.4(3)(a) – supply, or the offering to supply, by a defendant themselves.

Supply

The House of Lords in *Maginnis*[157] determined that whilst s.37(1) of the 1971 Act provides that the word supply, includes 'distribution' – it should also take its ordinary meaning, and be determined by reference to the context within which the behaviour occurred. That being said, it is still a somewhat convoluted situation; Lord Keith stated;

> *The word 'supply', in its ordinary natural meaning, conveys the idea of furnishing or providing to another something which is wanted or required in order to meet the wants or requirements of that other. It connotes more than the mere transfer of physical control of some chattel or object from one person to another.*[158]

In *Martin*[159] Lord Thomas CJ, summarised the position in an exceptionally straightforward way, in respect of the word 'supply' he said;

---

157   [1987] AC 303
158   Ibid, at [309]
159   (Dwain) & Anor [2015] 1 WLR 588

> *The word "supply" is a broad term. It does not by any stretch of the imagination result in a confinement to the expressions "actual delivery" or "past supply". It refers to the entire process of supply. In the present case there was clear evidence that the drugs were en route from London to Portsmouth. They were being transported so that they could be delivered to others in the Portsmouth area. It seems to us that that falls plainly within the word "supply".*

I would encourage readers to read the word supply in accordance with the provision in *Martin*, whilst Lord Keith in *Maginnis* determines the issue perfectly validly, the Lord Chief Justice's *dicta* in *Martin* is perhaps more reflective of a straightforward interpretation.

Offering to Supply

An offer to supply does not need to be a real offer, or even an offer which is achievable. The 'offering' variant of the offence is complete as soon as an offer is made.

In *Prior*[160], Auld LJ expressed the Court of Appeal's approval with a jury direction in the following terms; *"the jury that they should look at the words spoken and the circumstances in which they were spoken and decide for themselves whether they amounted to offers"*.[161]

Possession of a controlled drug with intent to supply

Possession with intent to supply, is an offence in its own right, but can be seen as a variant of the simple possession offence but accompanied by a *mens rea* to commit a further, more serious offence (supply). This offence combats situations whereby a

---

160 [2004] EWCA Crim 1147
161 Ibid, at [36]

dealer is caught at a stage where he is prepared to deal and intends to do so but has not actually done so – though of course it can encompass other acts and situations. Readers should note, if a person was to buy a controlled drug to share with their friends, regardless of payment being made or not, they would commit an offence under this provision.

The offence is contrary to s.5(3) of the 1971 Act, it references s.4(1)(b) of the same Act, which itself pronounces supplying a controlled substance to another as unlawful (see above).

s.5(3) states;

> *..., it is an offence for a person to have a controlled drug in his possession..., with intent to supply it to another in contravention of section 4(1) of this Act.*

Hence, where a person in possession of a controlled drug (the possessor), has a specific intention, to supply the thing in his possession[162] (which is, in fact, a controlled drug) – i.e., they intend to commit the full supply offence (under s.4(1))– they will commit an offence.

Simplified, and represented mathematically;

Simple Possession (s.5(2)) + Specific Intent to supply = Possession with intent (s.5(3))

---

162 *Wright* [2011] Cr App R 15

CHAPTER 9

Offences Against Public Order

Affray
s.4A Public Order
s.5 Public Order

The criminal law, as mentioned in chapter one of this text, draws a balance between personal autonomy, and the welfare of society. Public Order offences are one of the sub-classifications of offences which give rise to, perhaps, the most finely balanced situation in this regard. They do not require, on the whole, an injured party, and generally the 'victim' is considered to be the situation within which the offence is committed. In a wide sense, public order offences are offences where a defendant goes beyond the accepted norms of society, even where there is often no, specific, victim.

Affray

By way of the Public Order Act 1986, s.3(1);

> *A person is guilty of affray if he uses or threatens unlawful violence towards another and his conduct is such as would cause a person of reasonable firmness present at the scene to fear for his personal safety.*

Note, the word *"would"* in s.3(1), it is clear that the 'other' which is subjected to unlawful violence, or threatened with it, need not fear for his own personal safety – but neither does anyone else. The relevant 'victim' for an offence of affray is hypothetical – the *"person of reasonable firmness present at the scene"*.

The hypothetical person does not even have to be a 'likely' onlooker[163], nor does the offence have to take place in public.[164]

It is clear therefore that the offence of Affray has an exceptionally wide scope in law. However, the Affray offence should only be charged in circumstances where the offending behaviour causes a *serious* disturbance to the public order of things.[165]

---

163 Public Order Act 1986, s.3(4)
164 Public Order Act 1986, s.3(5)
165 *Davison* [1992] Crim LR 31

In *Thind*[166] the Court of Appeal outlined that it considered to be the three fundamental, elements of Affray;

(a) the use or threat of violence by a defendant
(b) against another person
(c) which would cause a third person to fear for their own safety.

Readers should be clear that the 'third' person does not need to be present, nor identifiable, nor actually fear for their own safety – they are entirely hypothetical, as earlier outlined.

Violence

By virtue of s.8(a) of the 1986 Act, the 'violence' must be against a person, violence against property will not suffice – in respect of a charge of Affray, for other purposes violence against property will suffice. By s.8(b) there is no requirement that the 'violence' is intended, or actually does, cause injury or damage – the Act provides an example of the throwing of a missile which falls short, satisfying the requirement for violence. Hence, 'violence', so long as it is against persons (on a charge of Affray), is given a wide meaning.

Use or threat of violence

Lord Bingham CJ, in *Smith*[167], gave an indicative (but not exhaustive) list of actions which may give rise to an offence of Affray, he said that Affray involves; *"a group of people who may well be shouting, struggling, threatening, waving weapons, throwing objects, exchanging and threatening blows and so on"*[168]

A threat, by way of s.3(3), cannot be made by words on their own. There is a requirement that there by some conduct on the

---

166 [1999] Crim LR 842
167 *(Christopher Floyd)* [1997] 1 Cr App R 14
168 Ibid, at p. 16

part of the defendant, thus making Affray a conduct crime. To that end, in the submission of the author, the word 'threat' cannot take its own everyday meaning – as a mere 'threat' could be satisfied by words alone, so 'threat' in the context of s.3 of the 1986 Act, must be a 'conducted threat'.

By way of an illustration; in *Dixon*[169] the defendant ordered their dog to attack a victim, the combination of the order and the attack itself gave rise to the fear of the hypothetical bystander – hence, the defendant was convicted of Affray. If the order had been given, but the dog had not responded, then there would be no affray, as the 'threat' would have been by words alone, and hence, not capable of being considered a 'conducted threat' for the purposes of s.3.

In *I*[170] the court concluded that the carrying of dangerous weapons, could, in the right circumstances be considered a 'threat' of unlawful violence, but, that question is ultimately one for the tribunal of fact.

Another

The person towards which the conducted threat is made must, in fact, be present at the scene of the Affray. The making of a threat towards a person not actually there, will not give rise to an Affray.

Lord Hutton, said;

> *"the present case demonstrates that a person should not be charged with the offence [of affray] unless he uses or threatens unlawful violence towards another person actually present at the scene and his conduct is such as would cause fear to a notional bystander of reasonable firmness."*[171]

---

169 [1993] Crim LR 579
170 *I v DPP* [2001] UKHL 10
171 Ibid, at [28], per Lord Hutton

Causing a person of reasonable firmness, present at the scene, to fear for their safety

The law is clear, the relevant test in relation to this element of the Affray offence, is wholly objective. It places a notional bystander in the room, or place, where the threat or use of violence against another is carried out – if that notional bystander would, reasonably, fear for their personal safety, then the element will be satisfied.

In *Leeson*[172] the court, quashing the defendant's conviction, held that if it would be impossible for the notional bystander to fear for their safety there can be no affray. In this case, the defendant threatened to kill their partner, whilst holding a knife – it is clear there was a conducted threat, but, as the issues were between a couple, the court found that there was no possibility of the notional bystander being placed in the relevant fear – hence no Affray.

It helps to be reminded that the offence of Affray is to protect the hypothetical bystander, as an offence contrary to public order, as opposed to an offence against a person. Whilst account can be taken of the reactions of bystanders actually present, it is only the reaction of the theoretical bystander that matters for the purposes of the s.3 offence.[173]

Mens Rea

By virtue of s.6 of the 1986 Act, affray is a crime of basic intention, or knowledge, as to the use of, or threat of, violence only. There is no need for the defendant to consider the notional bystander.

---

172 *Leeson v DPP* [2010] EWHC 994 (Admin)
173 *DPP v Cotcher* (1992) *The Times*, 29 December 1992

s.4A Public Order

By virtue of s.4A of the 1986 Act, a person will commit an offence, if, with the specific intent to cause a person harassment, alarm or distress, he;

> (a) uses threatening, abusive or insulting words or behaviour, or disorderly behaviour, or
> (b) displays any writing, sign or other visible representation which is threatening, abusive or insulting,
>
> thereby causing that or another person harassment, alarm or distress.

This requires the combination of the specific intention to cause another harassment, alarm or distress, a trigger behaviour, and the realisation of the specific intention.

The specific intention is governed by the ordinary principles of *mens rea*.

Harassment, Alarm or Distress

There is no formal, trifecta, definition of Harassment, Alarm or Distress but they are considered to be relatively serious consequences, it is submitted that a person must be more than merely offended. In R[174] Toulson J (as he then was), said of the trifecta;

> *"They are relatively strong words befitting an offence which may carry imprisonment or a substantial fine. I would hold that the word "distress" in this context requires emotional disturbance or upset. The statute does not attempt to define the degree required. It does not have to be grave but nor should the requirement be trivialized. There has to be something which amounts to real emotional disturbance or upset."*

---

174   *R (R) v DPP* [2006] EWHC 1375 (Admin)

Trigger Behaviours

The offence is made out, when with intent, a defendant undertakes a 'trigger behaviour' which causes harassment, alarm or distress. Those trigger behaviours, take their own everyday meaning, and should not be over complicated. They are;

- Using threatening words
- Using abusive words
- Using insulting words
- Using threatening behaviour
- Using abusive behaviour
- Using insulting Behaviour
- Using disorderly behaviour
- Displaying a writing which is threatening
- Displaying a writing which is abusive
- Displaying a writing which is insulting
- Displaying a sign, or other visible representation, which is threatening
- Displaying a sign, or other visible representation, which is abusive
- Displaying a sign, or other visible representation, which is insulting

Rude or offensive words are not always insulting[175], but they can be. By way of an illustration, in *Humphrey*[176] the defendant called the victim, an Asian man, as a *"fucking Islam"*, it is accepted that this, as the court found, is profoundly abusive. But it is likely that the words, taken separately, would not be; "fucking" is not a particularly nice word, however, it's common usage in parlance in modern times weakens the possibility

---

175 *Ambrose* (1973) 57 Cr App R 538
176 *R (DPP) v Humphrey* [2005] EWHC 822 (Admin)

that it would be found on its own facts, to be insulting unless combined with other factors, such as in *Humphrey*.

Place of commission

By s.4A(2) of the 1986 Act;

> *An offence under this section may be committed in a public or a private place, except that no offence is committed where the words or behaviour are used, or the writing, sign or other visible representation is displayed, by a person inside a dwelling and the person who is harassed, alarmed or distressed is also inside that or another dwelling.*

Private gardens[177] and Police Cells[178], are not considered dwellings.

Bespoke defences

By way of s.4A(3) of the 1968 Act, a defendant may have a bespoke defence to the offence under s.4A, where;

> *(a) that he was inside a dwelling and had no reason to believe that the words or behaviour used, or the writing, sign or other visible representation displayed, would be heard or seen by a person outside that or any other dwelling; or*
> *(b) that his conduct was reasonable.*

The 'reasonableness' defence, relates to Human Rights. Where a defendant is exercising his human rights (normally in relation to freedom of expression), and interference is not lawfully justified then the defendant will not commit an offence.

---

[177] *DPP v Distill* [2017] EWHC 2244 (Admin)
[178] *Francis* [2007] 1 WLR 1021

s.5 Public Order

A statutory offence requiring at least, the knowledge that the relevant offending behaviour may be threatening, abusive, or disorderly[179], s.5 public order is the lowest form of public order offence, it is only triable summarily, and has a maximum sentence of a fine. By virtue of s.5(1) of the 1986 Act, a person will be guilty of an offence if he;

> (a) uses threatening or abusive words or behaviour, or disorderly behaviour, or
> (b) displays any writing, sign or other visible representation which is threatening or abusive,
>
> within the hearing or sight of a person likely to be caused harassment, alarm or distress thereby.

The offence under s.5(1) mirrors that of s.4A, save for that the s.5(1) offence does not require that the defendant intended to cause a person harassment, alarm or distress. In essence here, the defendant must only, at the very least, be aware that his behaviour "might" be threatening, abusive or disorderly, there is no requirement for the prosecution to prove specific intention.[180]

In other substantive aspects the provisions which apply to s.4A, cross apply, to s.5.

Bespoke Defences

Like, s.4A(3), s.5(3) provides specific defences to a charge under s.5(1), they are;

---

179 Public Order Act 1986, s.6(4)
180 *DPP v Smith* [2017] EWHC 3193 (Admin)

> (a) that he had no reason to believe that there was any person within hearing or sight who was likely to be caused harassment, alarm or distress, or
> (b) that he was inside a dwelling and had no reason to believe that the words or behaviour used, or the writing, sign or other visible representation displayed, would be heard or seen by a person outside that or any other dwelling, or
> (c) that his conduct was reasonable.

By way of an illustration, in *Percy*[181] the defendant desecrated an American flag, outside a US Military base, within the UK, thereby causing distress to US service personnel and their families. The defendant appealed her conviction on the basis of 'reasonableness' under s.5(3)(c), the Court quashed her conviction on account that the Magistrates' Court had not placed sufficient weight to all the factors concerned. However, it is submitted that had the District Judge in the Magistrates' applied the correct weight the result could have been much different. The extent to which something is threatening, abusive, or, disorderly, is a matter which is highly fact-sensitive.

In other cases, the phrase *"Stop Immorality! Stop Homosexuality! Stop Lesbianism!"*[182] and *"Islam out of Britain"*[183] were both found to be unreasonable. Some may say that these phrases are just as 'abusive' as the conduct in *Percy*.

---

181 *DPP v Percy* [2001] All ER (D) 387 (Dec)
182 *Hammond v DPP* [2004] EWHC 69 (Admin)
183 *Norwood v DPP* [2003] EWHC 1564 (Admin)

CHAPTER 10

Driving & Road Traffic Offences

Dangerous Driving

Careless, and inconsiderate, Driving

Driving offences are some of the most commonly prosecuted offences in England and Wales, they are a significant portion of the diet of the Magistrates' Court. In this chapter two of the most common and well-known, conduct, offences are considered. But readers should make no mistake that Road Traffic Offences, are wide ranging, and there is an offence for almost every conceivable 'wrongdoing' that occurs on the road. Ultimately this is in view of the risks that the operation of motor vehicles and roadways carry. But it is submitted, the law in this area could be significantly more 'straightforward', whilst maintaining the level of protection it currently affords.

Dangerous Driving

Dangerous driving is a statutory offence, contrary to the Road Traffic Act 1988, s.2, which simply provides that;

> *A person who drives a mechanically propelled vehicle dangerously on a road or other public place is guilty of an offence.*

The offence can therefore be considered one of strict liability, there is no requirement that the driver should intend their driving to be dangerous, nor need they even be aware that their driving 'might' be dangerous. *"Proof of guilt depends on an objective standard of driving, namely, what would have been obvious to a competent and careful driver"*.[184]

The offence under s.2, therefore, can be broken down into four elements;

- Drives
- Mechanically propelled vehicle
- Dangerously
- On a road, or other, public place

---

184 *Loukes* [1996] 1 Cr App R 444

Drives

By virtue of the interpretation section (an intrinsic aid), the following definition is provided;

> *"driver", where a separate person acts as a steersman of a motor vehicle, includes ... that person as well as any other person engaged in the driving of the vehicle, and "drive" is to be interpreted accordingly,*

In essence, this means that 'drive' is given its ordinary and everyday meaning, for the purposes of s.2, hence, this is not a particularly complex requirement.

Mechanically propelled vehicle

There is no definition within the act which addresses this point. Pragmatically, it is question of fact for the court to determine whether something is a mechanically propelled vehicle. Generally, again, the courts do not find difficulty with this.

Dangerously

This is often the focus of cases of alleged dangerous driving, the defendant, if they accept being the driver, will say they were not *'dangerous'*.

Dangerous driving is defined by s.2A(1) of the 1988 Act, a person will drive dangerously if;

> ... a person is to be regarded as driving dangerously if ... —
> (a) the way he drives falls far below what would be expected of a competent and careful driver, and
> (b) it would be obvious to a competent and careful driver that driving in that way would be dangerous.

The use of the word *"far"* in s.2A(1)(a), is important. Dangerous driving is a serious offence, which carries a hefty sentence. It must be proven that the standard of driving fell 'far' enough below the standard to be dangerous.[185] This is similar in approach to the difference between 'negligence' and 'gross negligence' for the purposes of Gross Negligence Manslaughter.

Driving will also be dangerous if *"it would be obvious to a competent and careful driver that driving the vehicle in its current state would be dangerous."*[186] The 'current state' of the vehicle includes things attached to, or carried on, or, within, the vehicle.[187]

Dangerousness is considered by reference to *"danger either of injury to any person or of serious damage to property"*.[188] Only if such specific 'danger' is proven can the defendant be said to have been driving dangerously.

The caselaw in respect of dangerousness is voluminous and varied; it is particularly fact specific. Evidence of dangerous driving includes; using a mobile phone to film-events or take photographs[189], failing to stop or trying to escape police[190].

In respect of vehicles in dangerous states, the 'state' must be obvious to the careful and competent driver. This does not mean that they have been noticed by such a driver, but that they would be discoverable, on an inspection falling something between *"a fleeting glance"* and, *"a long look"*.[191] I.e., not only discoverable by the taking of further investigations or inspections, beyond that of the 'first glance'.[192]

---

185 *Jeshani* [2005] EWCA Crim 146
186 Road Traffic Act 1988, s.2A(2)
187 Road Traffic Act 1988, s.2A(4)
188 Road Traffic Act 1988, s.2A(3)
189 *DPP v Barreto* [2019] EWHC 2044 (Admin)
190 *Cooksley* [2003] EWCA Crim 996
191 *Marsh* [2002] EWCA Crim 137
192 *Strong* [1995] Crim LR 428

Road or another public place

In respect of roads, s.192 of the 1988 Act defines 'road' as; *"... any highway and any other road to which the public has access and includes bridges over which a road passes"*. Further, footpaths and bridleways are included in the statutory definition of a road, by virtue of s.34(1)(b) of the 1988 Act.

The leading authority on 'other road' within the meaning of s.192, is that of *Clarke v Kato*[193], where Lord Clyde outlined that;

> *"One obvious feature of a road as commonly understood is that its physical limits are defined or at least definable. It should always be possible to ascertain the sides of a road or to have them ascertained ... It may be continuous, ... or it may come to a termination, ... it is also necessary to consider the function of the place in order to see if it qualifies as a road. Essentially a road serves as a means of access."*

Ultimately, whether something that is not a 'highway' is an 'other road' will be a question of fact for the court to consider. It is submitted however that, ultimately, the question will be a relatively straightforward one for the court.

It is noteworthy though, that a clearly defined car park, will not be considered a 'road'.

Alternatively, the crown can pursue 'the other public place' element, of the offence, as opposed to the 'highway or other road' element. A public place does not have a definitive definition in law, but is a place to which the public has access, but this factor alone is not determinate.

In *Brown v Fisk & Ors*[194], Master Dagnall carefully examined a number of Criminal Law authorities relating to the provisions of what is a 'public place' within the meaning of the 1988 Act. He considered that, ultimately, the question was one of fact, considering the type of place, the use to which it was subject,

---

193 [1998] 4 All ER 417
194 [2021] EWHC 2769 (QB)

and whether it was the general public who had access, or a 'special class' of the public.

Careless, and inconsiderate, Driving

Careless driving is often referred to as 'driving without due care and attention", but the offences are technically referred to as 'Careless driving' or 'Inconsiderate driving' s.3 of the 1988 Act creates two separate offences. In order to be convicted a defendant need only commit either, careless, or, inconsiderate driving.

For discussion in relation to 'drives', 'mechanically propelled vehicle' and 'road or other public place' – readers should note that the same law applies above for dangerous driving as applies to the offence now discussed.

By virtue of s.3 of the 1988 Act;

If a person drives a mechanically propelled vehicle on a road or other public place without due care and attention, or without reasonable consideration for other persons using the road or place, he is guilty of an offence.

Further, s.3ZA provides;

A person is to be regarded as driving without due care and attention if (and only if) the way he drives falls below what would be expected of a competent and careful driver.

And, s.3ZA(4), provides;

A person is to be regarded as driving without reasonable consideration for other persons only if those persons are inconvenienced by his driving.

Readers will see from the above provisions that this offence only requires a driver to either, fall below the standard of a reasonably competent and careful driver (careless driving), or, in the alternative, inconvenience others by his driving (inconsiderate driving).

Again, the acid-tests for the above elements are fact specific, and objective, however, there are a few examples that have been given over the years as being indicative of careless, and inconsiderate, driving.

Careless Driving	Inconsiderate Driving
• 'rear-ending' a stationary vehicle[195] • Crossing relevant road markings[196] • Filming or taking photos[197]	• Inappropriately occupying the lane another is using[198] • Driving with undipped headlights[199] • Driving through a puddle causing pedestrians to be splashed[200]

---

195 *DPP v Parker* [1989] RTR 413
196 *Mundi v Warwickshire Police* [2001] EWHC Admin 448
197 *DPP v Barreto* [2019] EWHC 2044 (Admin)
198 *Waller v CPS* [2018] EWHC 3303 (Admin)
199 CPS Charging Guidance on Road Traffic Offences
200 Ibid

CHAPTER 11

Offences Involving Animals

A Brief History of Animal Crime Laws

Introduction to the Animal Welfare Act 2006
    'Protected Animals'
    Responsibility for Animals

Unnecessary Suffering
    S4(1) – Causing Unnecessary Suffering
    What is Meant by 'Suffering'?
    What is Meant by 'Unnecessary' Suffering?
    Ought to Have Known, or Ought Reasonably to Have Known
    S4(2) – Persons with Responsibility Allowing Another to Cause Unnecessary Suffering

Mutilation

Docking of Dogs' Tails

Administration of Poisons
    S7(1) – Administration of Poisons
    S7(2) – Administration of Poisons by Another Person

Animal Fights and Related Activities
    Animal Fighting Activities
    Animal Fighting and Video Recordings

The Welfare Offence

A Brief History of Animal Crime Laws

This chapter will deal with offences relating to animals, with a particular focus on the Animal Welfare Act 2006. Whilst there have been numerous examples of the criminal law being used throughout history in medieval 'animal trials',[201] it is only relatively recently, in the early 1800s, that the first pieces of legislation designed to *protect* animals were brought before the House of Commons.

Though the first few attempts at legislation were unsuccessful,[202] in 1822 Martin's Act was passed.[203] This Act made it an offence to *'wantonly and cruelly beat, abuse, or ill-treat any Horse, Mare, Gelding, Mule, Ass, Ox, Cow, Heifer, Steer, Sheep, or other Cattle'*. The penalty for this, if convicted, was a fine of no less than ten shillings and no more than five pounds.[204]

Eventually, Martin's Act was repealed and over the next 200 years, animal welfare legislation evolved, adapted and changed. Various pieces of criminal law legislation now exist to help protect animal welfare, with two of the most well-known pieces of legislation in the UK being the Animal Welfare Act 2006 and the Dangerous Dogs Act 1991. In this chapter, we will focus our attention on the various offences found under the Animal Welfare Act 2006.

---

201 Peter Dinzelbacher, 'Animal Trials: A Multidisciplinary Approach' [2002] 32(3) *The Journal of Interdisciplinary History* 405-421
202 For example, the 1800 & 1802 Bull Baiting Bills were argued to be necessary due to bull baiting being cruel and encouraging disorderly conduct amongst those who enjoyed it as a pastime, there was deep opposition to these Bills and they were considered to be meddlesome and unnecessary.
203 Formally titled 'An Act to prevent the cruel and improper Treatment of Cattle', but often referred to as 'Martin's Act'.
204 *Ibid*

Introduction to the Animal Welfare Act 2006

Upon enactment, the Animal Welfare Act 2006 repealed the Protection of Animals Act 1911 to protect the welfare of *'protected animals'* in the UK. This Act was largely seen as a positive addition to the law, due to its proactive rather than reactive nature. The Animal Welfare Act 2006 now ensures that the relevant authorities can act in advisory and educational capacities for those in charge of protected animals and, should this advice not be followed (or should an animal's needs not be met adequately), allows for prosecution or other legal action (such as formal warnings) before any suffering can befall an animal.

'Protected Animals'

The Animal Welfare Act 2006, firstly, defines an 'animal' as any vertebrate other than man and does not apply to any animals in the *'foetal or embryonic form'*, or to any invertebrate.[205] The Act further introduces the concept of what is referred to as a *'protected animal'*.

Under s2, an animal is deemed to be a *'protected animal'* if;

> (a) *it is of a kind that is commonly domesticated in the British Islands*
> (b) *it is under the control of man whether on a permanent or temporary basis, or*
> (c) *it is not living in a wild state.*

With this in mind, pets would fall under this definition, as would animals that are commonly domesticated as pets but that are stray or feral (e.g., dogs and cats). In addition to this, animals kept in captivity such as zoo animals, farm animals and animals that have been living under the control of humans but have recently escaped, for example, will also fall under this

---

205 S1(1-2) Animal Welfare Act 2006

definition. Wild animals not under the control of a human, such as foxes and badgers, are not ordinarily protected by this Act, however if such animals have been captured or rescued, the Act will apply to them for as long as they remain in care or captivity.

Responsibility for Animals

Before moving onto the substantive offences in this Act, it is first important to discuss the Act's use of the word *'responsibility'*. This concept is relatively straightforward, as s3 stipulates that persons will be deemed *'responsible'* for an animal if they have either temporary or permanent control of an animal (including being in charge of the animal) or if they own an animal (e.g. the owner of a pet, or a farmer who owns livestock).[206]

If the person in charge of an animal is under the age of 16, the person who is deemed to have *'actual care and control'* of the minor in question will be seen to be *'responsible'* for the relevant animals. Generally, this would usually be the parent or guardian of the minor in charge of the animal.[207]

Unnecessary Suffering

Of all the offences found in the Animal Welfare Act 2006, readers will most likely be familiar with s4 of this Act: the provision that deals with the offence of Unnecessary Suffering. The Unnecessary Suffering offence is found in s4(1) and s4(2) and extends to both omissions as well as positive acts.

S4(1) – Causing Unnecessary Suffering

Unnecessary suffering under s4(1) is as follows;

---

[206] S3(1-3) Animal Welfare Act 2006
[207] *Ibid*, s3(4)

> *(1) A person commits an offence if –*
> *(a) an act of his, or a failure of his to act, causes an animal to suffer,*
> *(b) he knew or ought reasonably to have known, that the act, or failure to act, would have that effect or be likely to do so,*
> *(c) the animal is a protected animal, and*
> *(d) the suffering is unnecessary.*

Readers should note that this offence does not amount to a general duty of care between the public and animals. For example, if a person was to see a stray dog running around their neighbourhood with an injured leg, the person would not be placed under a duty under s4(1) to provide care for this dog. This would be the case if the individual was an unrelated bystander, however, if the person was responsible for the dog's injury, then a duty may be imposed.

So, in terms of the *actus reus*, the requirements for this offence can be broken down into the following parts:

> A person responsible for a protected animal, either by an act or an omission, must cause an animal to suffer unnecessarily.

What is Meant by 'Suffering'?

To understand this offence, we must firstly consider what is meant by the term 'suffering'. This offence extends to both physical and mental suffering,[208] though this is not defined by the Act, meaning that in practical terms the determination of what constitutes mental or physical suffering is made by the court.[209]

---

208 S62(1) Animal Welfare Act 2006
209 *Bandeira and Brannigan v RSPCA* [2000] CO 2066/99

For example, in the recent case of *DM*,[210] an individual with mental health problems was sentenced to 24 months' imprisonment for multiple offences of both child neglect and causing Unnecessary Suffering under s4(1) to protected animals. The Defendant had two children and six dogs that were living in squalid and unsafe conditions. Five of the dogs found at the property were malnourished, neglected and in poor health, whilst a sixth dog was found to have been partially eaten alive by two of the other dogs and suffered severe injuries, leading to the dog being euthanised.

Whilst the physical suffering of these animals – and in particular the dog that had been partially eaten alive – was undoubtedly severe, both the physical and mental suffering of the dogs was taken into account when sentencing and Norton J deemed the suffering of the dog that had been partially eaten to fall into the top category for both harm and culpability with this in mind.[211]

The caselaw has confirmed, perhaps somewhat controversially, that the painless killing of an animal does not constitute suffering for this offence. For example, in *Isted*,[212] a keeper of livestock shot a neighbour's dog in the head with cartridges typically used for shooting rabbits or pheasants. The shot peppered the dog's head and, whilst the dog survived, the injuries the dog suffered were deemed to constitute Unnecessary Suffering.

What is noteworthy in this case is that it was noted in the judgment that had the dog been killed instantaneously, no suffering would have occurred and, therefore, no offence would have been committed under s4(1).

---

210 [2023] EWCA Crim 150
211 *Ibid, per* Norton J at para 15
212 [1998] 162 J.P. 513

What is Meant by 'Unnecessary' Suffering?

Before moving on to consider the *mens rea* of this offence, it is prudent to consider what is meant by the term *'unnecessary'* suffering. The case of Ford v Wiley provides the basis for the modern principles enshrined in the Act regarding this.[213]

This case concerned a farmer using an extremely painful method of dehorning his oxen. In this case, Hawkins J posited that suffering must be carried out *'without necessity'* for it to constitute an offence, and that the infliction of suffering must be justified and reasonably proportionate to the motive for inflicting it, with this motive needing to be in pursuit of a *'legitimate objective'*.[214] Thus, if one is to inflict some degree of suffering on animal, it must be:

1. Necessary
2. Justifiable
3. Reasonably proportionate
4. In pursuit of a legitimate aim

For example, if a person was to take their cat to the vet to get a cancerous tumour surgically removed, the consequence of such an operation would undoubtedly be to cause the animal some amount of pain and therefore a degree of suffering. In this case, however, no offence would be committed as the suffering would be deemed to be necessary, justifiable and proportionate for the purposes of removing the cancerous tumour from the cat, which would be in pursuit of a legitimate aim.

These principles are confirmed and expanded upon in s4(3) of the Animal Welfare Act 2006, which posits various considerations to take into account in determining whether suffering is unnecessary.[215]

---

213 [1889] 23 QBD 203
214 *Ibid, per* Hawkins J at paras 218 & 219
215 S4(3)(a-e) Animal Welfare Act 2006

Ought to Have Known, or Ought Reasonably to Have Known

The *mens rea* of s4(1) requires the defendant to have known, or to have ought reasonably to have known, that their conduct would cause an animal to suffer unnecessarily. This has been deemed to be an objective test that does not take into account the intentions of the defendant and covers both acts and omissions, as stated above.[216]

No offence is committed if, for example, the defendant had an honest and reasonable belief that their actions (or lack thereof) were necessary or beneficial to the animal's welfare. Furthermore, no offence is committed when the defendant was not aware of the incident that caused the animal to suffer unnecessarily.

However, this is not to say that a defendant can successfully claim ignorance of an animal's suffering as a defence in all situations. *Patterson v RSPCA* made it clear that persons responsible for protected animals have a duty to inspect these animals *'sufficiently regularly for conditions that would cause suffering to be brought to veterinary attention'*.[217]

S4(2) – Persons with Responsibility Allowing Another to Cause Unnecessary Suffering

S4(2) of the Animal Welfare Act 2006 involves the same considerations and principles as the above, the main difference being that this offence specifically criminalises a person responsible for a protected animal if they allow *another person* to cause the animal to suffer unnecessarily.

So, the offence is as follows;

---

216 *R (on the application of Gray and another) v Aylesbury Crown Court* [2013] EWHC 500 (Admin)
217 *Ibid, per* Blake J at para 35

> 2) A person commits an offence if —
>   (a) he is responsible for an animal,
>   (b) an act, or failure to act, of another person causes the animal to suffer,
>   (c) he permitted that to happen or failed to take such steps (whether by way of supervising the other person or otherwise) as were reasonable in all the circumstances to prevent that happening, and
>   (d) the suffering is unnecessary.

Thus, s4(2) relates to when individuals permit, either via a positive act or omission, another person to cause unnecessary suffering to an animal.

For example, in *Riley v Crown Prosecution Service*, multiple Appellants appealed against their conviction of a s4(2) offence.[218] These Appellants were partners of a slaughterhouse and were prosecuted on the basis that their failure to prevent their employees' improper handling of a cow due to be slaughtered amounted to Unnecessary Suffering. In this case, whilst the Appellants themselves did not cause this suffering, their failure to prevent it from taking place led to the completion of this offence.

Mutilation

The following two offences – Mutilation and Docking of Dogs' Tails – can be dealt with relatively quickly and are broadly similar offences.

Mutilations other than the docking of dogs' tails are prohibited under s5 of the Act. This section protects animals from 'prohibited procedures' involving the interference with sensitive tissues or bone structures of animals unless for medical treatment.[219]

---

218 [2016] EWHC 2531 (Admin)
219 S5(3) Animal Welfare Act 2006

An offence is also committed when a person with responsibility for an animal allows another person to carry out a prohibited procedure, failing to take reasonable steps to prevent this procedure from happening.[220]

For example, the cutting of a dog's ear, as is popular with breeds such as Dobermans, would fall under this section.

Docking of Dogs' Tails

The Docking of Dogs' Tails is a separate offence from Mutilation but bears much similarity to it.

This section makes it an offence to remove the whole or any part of a dog's tail for any reason other than for medical purposes. An offence is also committed when a person that has responsibility for an animal allows another person to do this in their stead.[221]

Administration of Poisons

Under s7(1) and s7(2) of the Animal Welfare Act 2006, it is an offence to administer poisonous or injurious substances to protected animals. This offence replaces the offence of Wilful Poisoning found in s1(1)(d) of the Protection of Animals Act 1911 and it is important to note that s7 does not cover cases of accidental poisoning. Both the administration of substances that are intrinsically poisonous, as well as substances that can be rendered poisonous via dosage, are covered by this section.

S7(1) – Administration of Poisons

The wording of s7(1) is as follows:

---

220 S5(2) Animal Welfare Act 2006
221 S6(1-2) Animal Welfare Act 2006

> *(1) A person commits an offence if, without lawful authority or reasonable excuse, he –*
> *(a) administers any poisonous or injurious drug or substance to a protected animal, knowing it to be poisonous or injurious, or*
> *(b) causes any poisonous or injurious drug or substance to be taken by a protected animal, knowing it to be poisonous or injurious.*

he *actus reus* for s7(1), therefore, is the direct administration of a *'poisonous or injurious'* substance to a protected animal, or the causing of such poisonous or injurious substances to be taken by the animal.

As opposed to the Unnecessary Suffering offence contained in s4, it is *not* necessary to show that an animal suffered as a result of the administration of poisons, but it *is* necessary to show that the defendant was aware that the substances administered were poisonous in nature.

Thus, the *mens rea* element of this offence requires intention, and the term *'administer'* should be interpreted as being a deliberate action.

S7(2) – Administration of Poisons by Another Person

The wording of s7(2) is as follows:

> *(2) A person commits an offence if –*
> *(a) he is responsible for an animal,*
> *(b) without lawful authority or reasonable excuse, another person administers a poisonous or injurious drug or substance to the animal or causes the animal to take such a drug or substance, and*
> *(c) he permitted that to happen or, knowing the drug or substance to be poisonous or injurious, he failed to take such steps (whether by way of supervising the other person or otherwise) as were reasonable in all the circumstances to prevent that happening.*

Whilst the *mens rea* element for s7(2) is the same as for s7(1), the *actus reus* in this section is slightly different.

S7(2) makes it an offence for an individual with responsibility for a protected animal to allow another person to administer a poisonous or injurious substance, whilst failing to take reasonable steps to prevent this. Thus, the *actus reus* for s7(2) is:

Responsibility for a protected animal + administration of poisonous/injurious substances by another person + a failure to take reasonable steps to prevent the administration.

The administration of a poisonous substance would not, however, amount to an offence if the defendant has a lawful or reasonable excuse to administer the substance in question. An obvious example would be the euthanasia of an animal – whilst the administration of euthanasia drugs would certainly amount to injurious/poisonous substances as they are designed to cause the death of the animal, no offence would be committed in this case provided that the euthanasia was carried out by a suitably qualified vet.

Animal Fights and Related Activities

S8 of the Animal Welfare Act criminalises both animal fighting and a range of other connected activities. S8(7) defines this as *'an occasion on which a protected animal is placed with an animal, or with a human, for the purpose of fighting, wrestling or baiting'*. Whilst the most common example of this is often dog fighting, this offence covers any animal that falls within the definition of a *'protected animal'*. So, for example, if a wild fox or other wild animal is captured with the intention of using it in an animal fight, that animal will be considered a protected animal for the duration of its captivity based on the definition found in s2 above.

S8 criminalises a range of different activities relating to fighting, wrestling or baiting animals and extends so far as to criminalise conduct such as possessing anything designed for use in connection with animal fighting, as well as supplying, publishing or even simply showing video recordings of animal fights to another.[222]

Animal Fighting Activities

The wording of s8(1-2) is as follows:

> (1) A person commits an offence if he —
>   (a) causes an animal fight to take place, or attempts to do so;
>   (b) knowingly receives money for admission to an animal fight;
>   (c) knowingly publicises a proposed animal fight;
>   (d) provides information about an animal fight to another with the intention of enabling or encouraging attendance at the fight;
>   (e) makes or accepts a bet on the outcome of an animal fight or on the likelihood of anything occurring or not occurring in the course of an animal fight;
>   (f) takes part in an animal fight;
>   (g) has in his possession anything designed or adapted for use in connection with an animal fight with the intention of its being so used;
>   (h) keeps or trains an animal for use for in connection with an animal fight;
>   (i) keeps any premises for use for an animal fight.
>
> (2) A person commits an offence if, without lawful authority or reasonable excuse, he is present at an animal fight.

It is therefore clear that s8(1-2) is aimed at criminalising various activities relating to animal fighting, including giving or receiving money in the form of bets and admission fees, promoting animal fights, providing information about animal fights with a view to encourage others to attend said fights,

---

222 S8(g) & s8(3)(a-c) Animal Welfare Act 2006

taking part in animal fights and, indeed, causing or attempting to cause an animal fight to take place.

The *mens rea* for this offence involves *'knowingly'* taking part in the above activities, and so it is clear that this offence is one of intention.

Animal Fighting and Video Recordings

S8(3) further expands this offence to include the following:

> (3) *A person commits an offence if, without lawful authority or reasonable excuse, he –*
> (a) *knowingly supplies a video recording of an animal fight,*
> (b) *knowingly publishes a video recording of an animal fight,*
> (c) *knowingly shows a video recording of an animal fight to another, or*
> (d) *possesses a video recording of an animal fight, knowing it to be such a recording, with the intention of supplying it.*

S8(3) therefore makes it an offence to supply, publish, show, or possess with intent to supply any video recordings without lawful authority or reasonable excuse. It is important to note, however, that an exemption applies here that can be found under subsection (5), exempting any video recordings used or intended for use in a *'programme service'*. The definition for this can be found in the Communications Act 2003 and refers to a *'service consisting in the provision of television programmes'*.[223] Moreover, videos taken outside of Great Britain or before the commencement date of the Animal Welfare Act 2006 will also not be covered by this section.[224]

The *mens rea* for this offence, again, involves intention as subsections (a), (b) and (c), state that the defendant must

---

223 Explanatory notes to the Communications Act 2003, para 458
224 S8(4)(a-b) Animal Welfare Act 2006

'knowingly' supply, publish or show a video recording of an animal fight. For subsection (d), the defendant must possess the video recording with the intention to supply it.

It is important to note that this offence is intended to apply to organised animal fights only. The animal fight cannot be due to a chance encounter, and so it cannot apply to situations such as taking an animal into the wilderness and releasing it in the hopes that it attacks another animal. The fight must, therefore, be a *'contrived or artificial creation specifically for the purpose'* of the fight and the other animal must be subject to some degree of constraint so that it had no natural means of escape.[225]

Furthermore, whilst many animal fights do involve the exchange of money in some capacity, this is not required for the commission of this offence, even though it may be an aggravating factor.[226]

As a final note on this offence, s8(1)(h) not only extends to those keeping and/or training animals for fighting purposes, but also to those who employ third parties (such as agents or trainers) for the same purposes. In *Wright v Reading Crown Court*,[227] the Appellant had been found guilty of an offence under s8(1)(h) after it was determined by the court that, despite the dog having been kept at another person's house for substantial periods of time, it was possible to keep or train an animal for fighting purposes through an agent.

The Welfare Offence

The final offence in the Animal Welfare Act 2009 can be found under s9 and is often referred to as the 'Welfare Offence'.

Under this section, a person commits an offence if:

---

225 *RSPCA v McCormick* [2016] EWHC 928 (Admin)
226 *Ibid*
227 [2017] EWHC 2643 (Admin)

> (1) ...he does not take such steps as are reasonable in all the circumstances to ensure that the needs of an animal for which he is responsible are met to the extent required by good practice.
> (2) For the purposes of this Act, an animal's needs shall be taken to include —
>   (a) its need for a suitable environment,
>   (b) its need for a suitable diet,
>   (c) its need to be able to exhibit normal behaviour patterns,
>   (d) any need it has to be housed with, or apart from, other animals, and
>   (e) its need to be protected from pain, suffering, injury and disease.
> (3) The circumstances to which it is relevant to have regard when applying subsection (1) include, in particular —
>   (a) any lawful purpose for which the animal is kept, and
>   (b) any lawful activity undertaken in relation to the animal.
> (4) Nothing in this section applies to the destruction of an animal in an appropriate and humane manner.

S9 is slightly different to the other offences covered in this chapter thus far, as it allows relevant authorities to act pro-actively instead of reactively. This duty extends to all persons who have responsibility for a protected animal, but does not extend protection to farmed animals, as the Welfare of Farmed Animals (England) Regulations 2007 deals with this instead.

S9(1) sets an objective standard for ensuring that those responsible for animals have a duty to care for them,[228] and there is often overlap between s4 – Unnecessary Suffering – and s9 due to the consequences of failing to care for an animal.

For example, if an animal suffers a cut on its leg and is not given proper veterinary attention and this cut then gets infected, firstly, the person responsible for the animal will likely be guilty of a s9(2)(e) offence. As the animal is likely to also suffer pain

---

[228] *Gray*, n.216

and distress as a result of the failure to get veterinary assistance and the injury worsening, this is also likely to constitute an offence under s4(1).

Similarly, if an animal is fed a healthy diet but otherwise is locked in an empty room all day with no stimulation, no human contact, no toys etc., the owner is likely to be guilty of an offence under s9(2)(a), (c) and perhaps (d). In addition to this, the animal is at the very least likely to experience mental suffering due to the lack of stimulation, and the person responsible for the animal would again be likely to be guilty of a s4(1) offence.

Whilst the test under s9 has been deemed to be an objective one, the courts have deemed it necessary in certain cases to consider not only whether the animals in question were given a reasonable standard of care, but also whether the defendant themselves acted reasonably in the circumstances.

R (RSPCA) v C provides a good example of this,[229] as in this case a 15-year-old girl was charged with an offence under s1 of the Protection of Animals Act 1911 by causing unnecessary suffering to her cat when she failed to seek appropriate veterinary care for it. Newman J stated that:

'The issue which the justices had to decide was whether or not this...girl had acted reasonably or unreasonably...[t]hat involved considering whether it was reasonable for her to go along with her father's view of the position, having regard to her age and position in the household, whether it was for her to take any other action, as she could have done, and whether it was reasonable or unreasonable for her to fail to take that other action.'[230]

Ultimately, the court held in this case that the girl's young age, and the fact that her father had advised her that her cat did not need any treatment (despite evidence to the contrary), must be taken into account.

---

229 [2006] EWHC 1069 (Admin)
230 *Ibid, per* Newman J at para 15

Whilst this case was brought under the Protection of Animals Act 1911 and cannot necessarily be used to reliably construe provisions under the Animal Welfare Act 2006,[231] based on the wording of s9 the judgment appears to be consistent with the principles contained within this section and so may still be considered good law.

---

[231] *Gray*, n.216

CHAPTER 12

Offences Involving Technology

Unauthorised Access Offence

Unauthorised Access Offence with intent to commit further offences

Unauthorised Access Offence

Hacking is a general term which incorporates a number of actions in everyday language. In law, however, the term 'hacking' is generally understood to be said in reference to an offence under the Computer Misuse Act 1990. It is this specific offence of 'unauthorised access' that this first section of this chapter will consider.

Under s.1 of the 1990 Act, a person will be guilty of an offence where;

> (a) *he causes a computer to perform any function with intent to secure access to any program or data held in any computer;*
> (b) *the access he intends to secure is unauthorised; and*
> (c) *he knows at the time when he causes the computer to perform the function that that is the case.*

It is noteworthy that no actual unauthorised access is required for a defendant 'hacker' to commit an offence under s.1. The act only requires a defendant to satisfy the requirements above, which, put simply, can be expressed as follows:

A defendant will commit an offence where he prompts a computer, intending to secure unauthorised access to either that computer, or another computer, directly or indirectly, and that computer responds, whilst the defendant knows his intended access is unauthorised, in some way, to the prompt from the defendant.

Further guidance on the interpretation of the s.1 offence, is contained within s.17 of the 1990 Act, which stipulates definitions in relation to the principles of 'securing access', 'unauthorised access' and, the position in relation to removable media.

Securing access

By virtue of s.17(2) of the 1990 Act;

> A person secures access to any program or data held in a computer if by causing a computer to perform any function he –
> (a) alters or erases the program or data;
> (b) copies or moves it to any storage medium other than that in which it is held or to a different location in the storage medium in which it is held;
> (c) uses it; or
> (d) has it output from the computer in which it is held (whether by having it displayed or in any other manner);

ss.17(3), 17(4), further elaborate on the definition in s.17(2), but the definition is relatively straightforward in nature, so it does not require further comment here.

Unauthorised Access

Pursuant to s.17(10), all references to a 'program' includes 'parts of a program'. Further, s.17(5) provides that;

> Access of any kind by any person to any program or data held in a computer is unauthorised if –
> (a) he is not himself entitled to control access of the kind in question to the program or data; and
> (b) he does not have consent to access by him of the kind in question to the program or data from any person who is so entitled...

Readers should note here that the use of the word 'and' in s.17(5) illuminates the fact that even if a person accessed data held in a computer without consent of the data owner, if that person is entitled to control access to the data concerned, then he will not commit an offence under s.1. Access will only be considered as unauthorised access if the elements of s.17(5)(a) and s.17(5)(b) are both satisfied.

Removable media

Under s.17(6);

> *References to any program or data held in a computer include references to any program or data held in any removable storage medium which is for the time being in the computer; and a computer is to be regarded as containing any program or data held in any such medium.*

The position at common law

Caselaw provides two distinct positions in relation to the offence under s.1. In the first case of *Bignell*[232] the court established that where a defendant causes another person to cause the function, but that person is authorised to access the computer system concerned there will be no offence under s.1. By way of context, in *Bignell* two police officers instructed a worker in the police control room to access the police national computer, for non-official reasons. As the officers had not 'caused the computer to perform a function' there could be no offence, as a key element of the *actus reus* was missing.

In the latter case of *Allison*[233], the House of Lords, confirmed the position in *Bignell*, saying, *inter alia*;

> *"it was a possible view of the facts that the role of the officers in Bignell had merely been to request another to obtain information by using the computer. The computer operator did not exceed his authority. His authority permitted him to access the data on the computer for the purpose of responding to requests made to him in proper form by police officers. No offence had been committed under section 1 of the CMA."*

---

232 [1998] 1 Cr App R 1
233 *R v Bow Street Magistrates' Court and Allison (AP) Ex Parte Government of the United States of America (Allison)* [2002] 2 AC 216

The Unauthorised Access offence is an offence of specific intention, as a defendant, in order to be convicted, must intend to gain access to any program or data, held in any computer. But further, the offence also requires the relevant knowledge, that at the time when a defendant causes the computer in question to perform the function in question, he must know that the access he intends to gain is, in fact, unauthorised.

Unauthorised Access Offence with intent to commit further offences

Parliament, by virtue of s.2 of the 1990 Act, create, almost, an aggravated form of the s.1 offence. Whereby a person commits the unauthorised access offence, whilst having, at the same time, and intention to commit or enable the commission of another, objectively more serious, specified offence.

The 1990 Act provides, in s.2;

> A person is guilty of an offence under this section if he commits an offence under section 1 above ("the unauthorised access offence") with intent—
> (a) to commit an offence to which this section applies; or
> (b) to facilitate the commission of such an offence (whether by himself or by any other person);
> and the offence he intends to commit or facilitate is referred to below in this section as the further offence.

The section then goes onto provide which offences, will be considered, as relevant 'further offences';

> (a) for which the sentence is fixed by law; or
> (b) for which a person who has attained the age of ... eighteen ... and has no previous convictions may be sentenced to imprisonment for a term of five years...

Notably, there is no requirement that the further offence will, in fact be committed, and, oddly, even if the further offence is impossible the s.2 offence will nevertheless, be able to be committed – contrary to more general principles of law.

CHAPTER 13

General Defences

Self Defence
Consent

The discussion in this chapter will surround the operation of defences to crimes. This text has already touched on some specific defences in relation to specific offences. Such as the partial defences to Murder, of loss of control, and of diminished responsibility, and, the bespoke defences incorporated into the Public Order Act.

This section will deal with some of the defences that can apply to many crimes. This section does not include all the relevant defences that law students may come across but does reference some of the more commonly understood defences, befitting this straightforward guide to criminal law.

Self Defence

The defence of 'self-defence' almost always relates to offences through which violence was used.[234] If this defence is successful what would, otherwise, be a criminal offence of violence will be considered to be a lawful action – even Murder. Where force is not used during the commission of the offence, it may be more appropriate to consider duress as an alternative defence.[235]

Self-defence is a defence of justification, it comes into being where a defendant seeks to justify their conduct due to a threat being made towards, normally, his own health or safety.

The defence has been in place since time immemorial, but the modern variation is encapsulated within various statutes, in addition to the common law.

Regardless of the provisions contained within the Criminal Justice and Immigration Act 2008, s.76, the defence of self-defence (which includes defence of another, and the defence (or protection) of property), is a defence a common law, and is principally governed by well-established principles of caselaw,

---

234 *Renouf* [1986] 2 All ER 449
235 *Symonds* [1998] Crim LR 280

which s.76 adds to – this addition relates to reasonableness and is covered below.

Further, the Criminal Law Act 1967, s.3(1), adds to the common law, a provision that states that;

> *A person may use such force as is reasonable in the circumstances in the prevention of crime, or in effecting or assisting in the lawful arrest of offenders or suspected offenders or of persons unlawfully at large.*

So, the defence operates successfully where a defendant uses force during the commission of an offence, in order to either defend themselves (another, or property), or, prevent crime, or, assist in a lawful arrest.

The question of purpose will generally be quite straightforward, albeit some specific provisions do apply, which are not considered in this text, but generally do align with common sense.

The central question when considering self-defence is generally whether or not the force used by the defendant, was reasonable.

By s.76(3) of the 2008 Act, where the question arises as to whether or not the force used by the defendant, was reasonable, the reasonableness is to be assessed by virtue of the circumstances as the Defendant themselves, genuinely, believed them to be.

Assessing Reasonableness

Once the court has ascertained what circumstances the defendant believed to be in existence, they must then consider the following factors;

- did the defendant have a mistaken belief in circumstances by way of his voluntary intoxication? If yes, then he cannot rely on that mistaken belief.[236]

---
236 Criminal Justice and Immigration Act 2008, s.76(5)

- If the defendant was a 'householder' (e.g., was defending himself in his own home), then his force need not be reasonable, but must not be grossly disproportionate.[237]
- In a non-householder case, the force must be proportionate.[238]
- Whether or not the defendant could have run away, as opposed to using force, should be considered – but the defendant does not have to run away.[239]
- A person cannot be expected to complete a fine balancing exercise in the heat of the moment as to the precise level of force required.[240]
- Evidence that a defendant only took steps that they honestly and instinctively thought were required is strong evidence of reasonableness.[241]
- Any other matters the tribunal of fact consider to be relevant to determining the reasonableness of a defendant's actions.[242]

To represent the defence of self-defence in a much simplified, mathematical, form;

Honest Belief of a need to defend + Use of Reasonable Force = Self-defence

Readers should note that Self Defence is a compete defence, if successful the defendant will be Not Guilty, but if it fails, there is no middle ground – the defendant will be convicted. It is 'all or nothing'.[243]

---

[237] Criminal Justice and Immigration Act 2008, s.76(5A)
[238] Criminal Justice and Immigration Act 2008, s.76(6)
[239] Criminal Justice and Immigration Act 2008, s.76(6A)
[240] Criminal Justice and Immigration Act 2008, s.76(7)(a)
[241] Criminal Justice and Immigration Act 2008, s.76(7)(b)
[242] Criminal Justice and Immigration Act 2008, s.76(8)
[243] *McInnes* [1971] 3 All ER 295

Consent

We have already considered consent in relation to sexual offences, and, to a lesser and more general extent, in respect of criminal damage. Discussion of consent here is more general still, but will focus, by the nature of the common law, on offences against the person.

Ultimately, consent in one form or another is a defence to many offences. It cannot be used as a defence to Murder, murder with consent would be akin to Euthanasia, which is an offence under English and Welsh law.

It is common knowledge that a person with capacity can consent or choose not to consent to certain activities, such as medical treatment or participating in intimate acts. But the law places limitations on when a person charged with a crime, can be absolved from culpability just because someone agreed to be subjected to a particular behaviour, that would generally be considered an offence.

Genuine Consent

The most obvious limitation on consent is where a defendant relies on the apparent consent of someone who did not have capacity to make the decision as to consent. In order to consent, the consenting party must be able to understand what it is they are consenting to. In *Burrell*[244] the Court considered that two children aged 12 and 13 did not understand the nature of a tattoo, and hence they could not consent – on that basis the Defendant, who admitted tattooing the boys, with their 'consent' was convicted of an offence of Assault occasioning Actual Bodily Harm[245].

Further, if the nature of the consent is understood, it must not have been corrupted by fraud, either in relation to the identity

---

244 *Burrell v Hammer* [1967] Crim LR 169
245 Offences Against the Person Act 1861, s.47

of the person whom the defendant consents with, or the nature and quality of the specific act consented to.

In *Richardson*[246] the defendant was a suspended dentist, not entitled to practice as a dentist. Yet she did, she was charged with ABH for the procedures, but the Court of Appeal held that, even though the defendant practised when not entitled, she had not informed the patients as to her identify – therefore the patient's consent was valid.

In *Tabassum*[247] an ICT professional pretended to conduct examinations on women, supposedly for medical purposes. It was established by the appeal court that in that case the women were consenting to the touching for medical purposes, and as that was not the true nature of the act, the consent was not valid as it had been vitiated by the fraud as to the nature and quality of the act.

What can a person consent to?

There are certain categories of consent that are generally accepted as being *prima facie* valid. They are;

- Injury during the course of properly conducted sports.[248]
- Surgery
- Cosmetic enhancements, such as ear piercings and tattoos[249]
- 'Horseplay' (jovial activities), Banter[250]

What can someone not consent to?

Generally, unless one of the above exceptions apply, a person cannot consent to injury which is at a level at, or above, that of ABH.

---

246 [1998] 2 Cr App R 200
247 [2000] 2 Cr App R 328
248 *Billinghurst* [1978] Crim LR 553
249 *Wilson* [1996] Crim LR 573
250 *Aitken* [1992] 1 WLR 1066

GENERAL DEFENCES

One of the main academic considerations here is in relation to harm caused for sexual gratification *'pain-play'*.

In *Brown*[251] Lord Templeman held that;

> "Society is entitled and bound to protect itself against a cult of violence. Pleasure derived from the infliction of pain is an evil thing. Cruelty is uncivilised."

Lord Lowry, went onto consider;

> "...the reason for the proposed exemption being that both those who will inflict and those who will suffer the injury wish to satisfy a perverted and depraved sexual desire. Sadomasochistic homosexual activity cannot be regarded as conducive to the enhancement or enjoyment of family life or conducive to the welfare of society."

The decision in *Brown* is widely, and it is submitted, rightly, criticised, by legal commentators, and professionals alike. Though the decision in Brown remains good law, it is submitted that should the question of 'pain-play' be brought before the courts again the outcome would be likely to be different, given changing societal attitudes since the early 1990s.

---

251 [1993] 2 All ER 75

FURTHER READING

In the preface to this text, I outlined that this book is to be treated as a springboard into further reading and/or study. To that end I have included three books below, that I personally recommend to students who I teach.

Mark Thomas' textbook is a fantastic resource for students who are studying Criminal Law at levels 4 and above, it provides a complete picture of the relevant information that, for reasons of practicality, was not explicitly included within this *Straightforward Guide*.

Blackstone's Criminal Practice is a practitioner's guide used by barristers throughout England and Wales, it is the preferred text for Bar Schools teaching criminal litigation and is my first port of call when reminding myself of concepts when I am designing teaching material and before I attend the lectures and seminars which I deliver.

Smith, Hogan and Ormerod's Criminal Law has long been the authoritative textbook on criminal law, it is often cited by appeal courts as a key source of academic commentary.

- Criminal Law by Mark Thomas, 3rd Edition, Hall & Stott Publishing. ISBN: 9781838166465
- Blackstone's Criminal Practice 2023, OUP. ISBN: 9780192870292
- Smith, Hogan, and Ormerod's Criminal Law, 16th Edition, OUP. ISBN: 9780198849704

Online Resources

From time to time, further resources will be added to www.cowburn.pro/sgcl, these resources will include worked examples of offences, further commentary, and relevant updates.

INDEX

Abnormality of mental functioning, 36, 37
Absence of defence crimes, 25
Acts of God, 22
Acts of the victim, 20
Acts of third parties, 21
Actual Bodily harm, 49
Actus Reus, 14
Administration of poisons, 132, 133
Affray, 106
Aggravated criminal damages, 95
Animal fighting activities, 134, 135
Animal fighting and video recordings, 134, 135
Animal Welfare Act 2006, 124, 125
Appropriation, 72
Apprehension of violence, 46
Arson, 95
Assault, 46, 54
Assault by penetration, 63
Assault Occasioning Actual Bodily Harm (ABH), 49, 50
Assessing reasonableness, 149
Autonomy, 8

Basic intent crimes, 24, 47
Battery, 47, 54
Blackstone's Criminal Practice, 22, 80
British Transport Police, 2
Burglary, 78

Careless, and inconsiderate, Driving, 120
Causation, 18
Causing death by driving, 42
Causing death by careless driving when under the influence of drink or drugs, 42
Causing unnecessary suffering (Animals), 126
Chief Crown Prosecutor, 3
Civil Nuclear Constabulary, 2
Common law offences, 2
Computer Misuse Act 1990, 142
Conduct crimes, 26
Conduct and result crimes, 26
Consent (General), 151
Constructive (Unlawful Act) Manslaughter), 38
Coroners and Justices Act 2009, 32
Contractual duties, 15, 16
Controlled Drug, 98
Conveyance, 88
Court of Appeal (Criminal Division), 1
CPS Proceeds of Crime Division (CPSPOC), 3
Criminal Appeal Act 1995, 4
Criminal appeals, 4
Criminal damage 1971, 92
Criminal Damage Act 1971, 92
Criminal Justice Act 1988, 46
Criminal Justice and Immigration Act 2008, 148

Criminal Law Act 1967, 148
Crown Court, 15
Crown Prosecution Service (CPS), 3
Cunningham recklessness, 20

Damage to property, 91, 92
Dangerous Dogs Act 1991, 22, 188
Dangerous driving, 124
Dangerousness, 39
Death by careless or inconsiderate driving, 41
Death by dangerous driving, 41
Diminished responsibility, 32, 35
Direct Intent, 23
Director of Public Prosecutions, 3
Dishonesty, 70
Disqualified drivers, 42
Distress, 84, 87
Docking of dogs' tails, 131, 132
Driving & road traffic offences, 116
Duties by special relationships, 15, 17

Elements of an Offence, 13
Entry, 79

Factual causation, 18
Fair labelling, 8
Fair warning, 7, 8
Fatal offences against the person, 28
Female genitalia, 57
Force, 48, 77
Fraud, 182
Fraud by abuse of position, 83
Fraud by false representation, 82, 83, 84

General consent, 60
General defences, 147
Genuine consent, 151
Grievous bodily harm (GBH), 31
Gross negligence manslaughter, 39

Hacking, 142
Harassment, 110
His Majesty's (HM) Courts and Tribunals Service (HMCTS), 3
Home Office, 13
Homicide Act 1957, 35

Immediacy, 47
Involuntary manslaughter, 38

Judicial Committee of the Privy Council, 39

Killing, 29
Kings peace, 30
Knowledge, 24

Legal causation, 20
Loss of self-control, 32 33

Magistrates' Courts, 5
Making off without Payment, 85
Malice of aforethought, 31
Martins Act 1822, 124
Mens Rea, 23, 108
Monarch's Peace, 30
Murder, 13, 28, 31
Mutilation (Animals), 131

Negligence, 24
Non-fatal offences against the person, 12

INDEX

Oblique Intent, 23, 31
Offences against public order, 106
Offences involving Animals, 123
Offences Involving Technology, 210
Offences of dishonesty, 70
Offences of Possession & Supply, 99, 103

Penile penetration, 57
Possession of a controlled drug, 98
Posession of a controlled drug with intent to supply, 99, 103
Prison adjudication, 4
Prisons, 4
Probation, 4
Principles of criminal law, 7
Property, 73
Prosecution of Offences Act 1985, 3
Protected animals, 123
Protection of Animals Act 1911, 139
Provocation, 32
Psychoactive Substances Act 2016, 98
Public order, 110, 113
Public Order Act 1986, 106

Rape, 56
Reasonable creature, 30
Rebuttable presumptions, 59
Recklessness, 23, 47
Recognised medical condition, 78
Removable media, 144
Responsibility for Animals, 126
Result crimes, 26
Road Traffic Act 1988, 116

Robbery, 76
RSPCA, 3

Self defence, 26, 147
Serious economic, organised crime, 3
Sexual assault, 65
Sexual Offences Act 2003, 56
Solicitor advocates, 6
Sources of criminal law, 12
Special Crime and Counter Terrorism Division, 3
Specific defence (Drugs), 100
Specific intent, 63
Specific intent crime, 24
Stare Decisis 12
Statutory duties, 49
Statutory offences, 15, 16
Strict liability, 25
Substantial impairment, 37
Supply of (or offering to supply) a controlled drug, 101
Supreme Court, 1, 6

Taking Conveyance without Authority 'TWOC', 87
The Criminal Cases Review Commission, 4
The High Court, 6
The welfare offence, 137
Theft Act 1978, 86
Theft Act 1988, 70
Theft, 70, 77
Trespasser, 80
Trigger behaviours, 111

Unauthorised Access offence (Technology), 142, 143
Unnecessary suffering (Animals), 126, 129

Unlawfulness, 28
Unlicensed drivers, 42
Uninsured drivers, 42

Vaginal penetration, 57
Violence, 107
Voluntary assumption, 15
Voluntary manslaughter, 32

Welfare, 9
Welfare of Farmed Animals (England) Regulations 2007, 136
With intention, 31
Wounding or inflicting grievous bodily harm, 50, 51